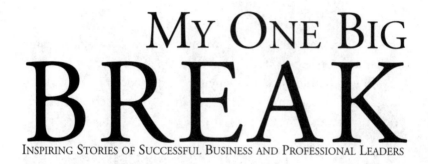

My One Big BREAK

Inspiring Stories of Successful Business and Professional Leaders

John E. Grimm III and Clark A. Johnson

with Rob Rains

ISBN: 1-58261-906-9

Publishers: Peter L. Bannon and Joseph J. Bannon Sr.
Senior managing editor: Susan M. Moyer
Developmental editor: Mark E. Zulauf
Art director: K. Jeffrey Higgerson
Dust jacket design: Dustin Hubbart
Layout design: Alicia Wentworth
Project manager: Kathryn R. Holleman
Imaging: Dustin Hubbart
Photo editor: Erin Linden-Levy
Vice president of sales and marketing: Kevin King
Media and promotions managers: Michael Hagan (regional),
    Randy Fouts (national), Maurey Williamson (print)

Printed in the United States of America

Spotlight Press L.L.C.
804 North Neil Street
Champaign, IL 61820

Phone: 1-877-424-2665
Fax: 217-363-2073
Web site: www.SpotlightPress.com

CONTENTS

INTRODUCTION

During their 40-plus years in the business world, Jack Grimm and Clark Johnson had the opportunity to relate with executives and professionals from varied industries around the world. Although they did not know each other during that time, they later found out they had many of the same questions about what determines the level of success an individual can achieve in the business world.

When Grimm and Johnson became acquainted a couple of years ago, they decided that, if they were interested in the topic, then maybe others were too. So they began asking friends and colleagues whether they had experienced a "big break" that had made the difference in their careers. Twenty-four of the first 25 people they asked said, "Oh, yes, and let me tell you about it."

It intrigued both men how some people could become successful, and others, with similar education and background, were never able to achieve the same high-level goals. Was the disparity due to a difference in intellect and ambition? Or was it "luck" that made the difference?

What they discovered was that one of the keys to success for many executives and professionals was that "one big break." For some it was a very dramatic moment they would remember the rest of their lives. For others it was a more gradual progression of events and opportunities, but still the factor that launched them on the way to future success.

What many of the leaders told the authors was that the key to their success was being prepared when their big opportunity happened, and being lucky enough to recognize it at the time to take full advantage of it.

The two decided to share these stories as inspiring examples to young men and women who are anticipating their own "big break." The authors have discussed with many current and former executives and professionals the factors involved in their formula for success. This book is the result of their efforts.

Both Grimm and Johnson, of course, have their own stories to tell about the "big break" in their careers.

JOHN E. GRIMM III

When I completed my navy service in 1946, I was hired by Macy's to work in their training program and later became a buyer. One of my assignments was as an assistant buyer in the music and record department. I left that job after a few years to become a product advertising manager in the consumer products division of the Borden Co.

I was working there when a friend took me to lunch one day and then back to his apartment to watch General Douglas MacArthur's speech to Congress. It turned out to become a very famous speech with the oft-quoted phrase, "Old soldiers never die, they just fade away." Like most Americans, I was deeply touched by the speech.

The next day I asked my father if he had heard the speech. He told me he had not because he had been in a meeting all day. I said, "I should have made a recording of it for you." Probably because of my background working in the record department at Macy's, the idea struck me that, if I could record a copy of the speech, maybe I could sell it to department and music stories. I thought people like my father, who had heard about the speech but had not heard it, would probably buy a copy.

My lawyer assured me there was no legal issue with recording the speech because it had been delivered in Congress and was

JOHN E. GRIMM III is chairman and CEO of Midbrook, Inc., a business consulting firm founded in 1985 following 24 years as corporate vice president of the Colgate-Palmolive Company. He served on the Rival Company board in Kansas City, Missouri, for five years until the company was sold. He is a former president and chairman of the Madison Square Boys and Girls Club in New York City and currently serves as the vice chairman of the Executive Committee, as well as vice president of the Southampton Hospital board and a member of the Skin Cancer Foundation board.

therefore considered public domain. So with the help of my former boss at Macy's, who committed to buying the records and placing them in his stores, overnight I succeeded in making a recording of MacArthur's speech. I placed an order for 10,000 33 1/3 RPM records of the speech with no money down. The same day I called the eight largest department stores in the country, taking orders for next-day delivery.

Macy's ran a large ad in the Sunday newspapers advertising the record for a cost of $3.95. By Tuesday it was the largest selling record for a two-day period in Macy's history. Of greater importance, *Life* and other magazines ran feature articles with the headline, "Amateur Scoops Record Industry."

Several months later I was interviewed for a job at Lever Brothers by Charles T. Lipscomb, president of the Pepsodent division. I had barely sat down when Lipscomb, a 6-foot-4, 250-pound mountain of a man, snapped, "Listen sonny, don't bother telling me you were president of your class, or captain of your baseball team. Just tell me what you've done better and different than anyone else."

At that point I didn't say anything but simply took out the two magazines, turned to the articles and politely placed them on the top of his desk.

He looked at them for a couple of minutes, stood up and said, "Come with me." We walked to the office of the vice president of sales, and Lipscomb said to him, "Hire him," and pointed to me. He then turned around and walked out of the office.

Charlie was truly my "one big break." Working with Charlie made a big difference in my career path. He was a great leader, highly respected by all those who knew him, and a valued friend. A few years later when the company was sold and we were both looking for a job, he recommended me to Sterling Drug, where I became corporate vice president. I left that job three years later to become a corporate vice president of Colgate-Palmolive Co. and worked there with various responsibilities for 24 years, eventually retiring in 1984.

I was fortunate that all four of my grandparents lived until I was 23 years of age. They were great role models. I've also been privileged to have had wonderful parents and two great brothers and one sister. Last but certainly not least, I have a lovely wife, Ann, who is my best friend—even though she is now beating me in golf.

As my father once advised me, "If you work 15 percent harder, longer and better than your cohorts, it will pay off 100 percent, because you will stand 15 percent higher and be recognized."

I don't know if any of my success would have been possible without taking the chance to make and sell recordings of General MacArthur's speech, and I doubt I would have ever thought of doing that without my background of working in the record department at Macy's. As the famous saying goes, luck is "when preparation meets opportunity" and that's when it happened for me.

1. Unless you have a great memory, always tell the truth.

2. Remember, you'll meet the same people going up the ladder that you will meet coming down.

3. Once you've learned how to do something, pass that knowledge on to others. Learn to teach.

4. Get involved in a charity as a leader. It takes more skill to lead and motivate people you don't pay and don't have the right to "hire and fire."

5. Gossip in a business or professional field is like a virus, it spreads rapidly and comes back to you.

6. As Dale Carnegie once said, "Will you help me?" is one of the most powerful requests a person can make. How can you say no?

CLARK A. JOHNSON

The first big break that would prove important to my future business career happened at the University of Iowa late in my freshman year.

I noticed a job posting in the marketing department for a vacation relief salesman at the Rath Packing Co. in Waterloo, Iowa. The summer position involved two weeks of training, then covering four sales territories for two weeks each, while the regular salesman was on vacation. It provided a company car, an expense account and paid $55 per week.

Qualifications for the position were that candidates had to have completed their junior year of college and be ranked in the top 20 percent of their academic class. I missed on both accounts. Additionally, there were 116 applications for the position. The placement officer at the university laughed at my chances.

I called for an appointment with the training director of the company anyway, took a bus the 125 miles to Waterloo and convinced them to hire me. This experience was great—it was here that I first learned the important life lessons to be aggressive and to always believe in yourself.

The major turning point in my business career and my life came 28 years later, in 1978, while working for the Wickes Corporation as a senior vice president. In three years I had taken

CLARK A. JOHNSON is the chairman of the board of PSS
World Medical, a health care distribution business. He retired
as chairman and CEO of Pier 1 Imports in 1998 after a 13-year
career with the company. He presently serves on seven corporate boards and makes his home with his wife, Joan, in Palm
Beach, Florida.

one of their poorest performing divisions from a $6 million to loss to a $15 million profit. As a reward, Wickes agreed to send me to the prestigious Harvard Business School's Advanced Management Program.

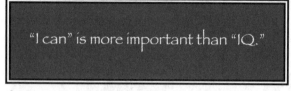

My class consisted of 161 CEOs and senior executives from companies around the world. Many of them had much more experience and education than I had. I compared myself to a Triple A baseball player being called up to the major leagues. I thought I had the talent to compete at that level, but could I really hit a major league curve ball?

I found out in late December that Wickes was sending me to the class, which started in February. When I called to enroll, I was told the class was full but I could attend the next year. Instead of accepting this outcome, I flew to Boston, rented a car, drove to Harvard and knocked on the director's door.

I told him getting into the class was the most important thing in my life and implored him, "If you give me a seat, I promise to be the best AMP student you've ever had. I will work the hardest and contribute to the knowledge of others." He let me in, and I followed through on my promise. At the end of the class, he shook my hand and said, "I guess you were right."

To my surprise, this impressive group of business leaders elected me class president. After interacting with them over a three-month period, I came away convinced I had the skills and ability to succeed at a top corporate level.

I returned to Wickes, but elevated my goal and set my sights on becoming a CEO of a major company. Had I not gone to Harvard I don't know if that would have happened. I knew I had the motivation, the work ethic and the integrity, along with the credibility from my associates. The Harvard experience also gave me the knowledge I could match up with other successful executives. That boost in confidence motivated me through the rest of my career.

I got my chance to become a CEO in 1985, when I joined Pier 1 Imports. During the 13 years I was there, the company grew from $170 million in annual sales to more than $1 billion a year, with 13,000 employees in 800 stores around the world.

The knowledge that I gained at Harvard helped make that success possible. My biggest challenge at Pier 1 was building a management team that brought together the right kind of personalities, aspirations and motivations to create the right culture to implement our corporate strategy. Corporate culture is nothing more than a set of shared beliefs about what the company can be and how the people in it should work together. The hard part is putting together a team that fits the desirable culture.

You overcome that challenge by staying cognizant of your organization's bench strength and being willing to take risks in your selection and promotion of people. I operated under the philosophy that "I can" beats "IQ." When you get highly motivated people who share your commitment to the company's goals and strategies and you turn them loose, they usually produce outstanding results.

Another key to success I learned over the years was to never back away from making a tough decision. We needed to install new cash registers throughout the Pier 1 system, which represented a $22 million investment. We put together a task force, which recommended an emerging vendor. Despite their impassioned presentation, I overrode the recommendation and selected IBM, a company I had worked with in the past and one I knew was supported by the best service in the industry. It seemed to me to be the safest choice.

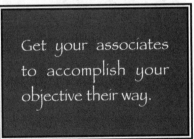

Get your associates to accomplish your objective their way.

The head of the task force—a person who was identified as having a bright future in the company—resigned in protest. While I hated to see him leave, I stood by my decision. As it turned out, a competitor purchased the other system for his company and incurred several million dollars in additional maintenance costs.

Perhaps the most important lesson I have learned over the years is to clearly define a strategy and stick with it. As a young man, I started out selling lumber and plywood in South Dakota. I did well because I made more calls and asked for more orders than anyone else, not because I had an understanding of the big picture. When I began running organizations, however, I found that to truly succeed you need to define your strategic goals and objectives in clear, understandable terms. More important, you succeed by making certain everyone in a key position agrees with the goals and accepts them as their own. My experience at Pier 1 taught me about the importance of not changing your tactics and goals every time you suffer a minor setback.

Successful CEOs, I have found, are able to fend off their critics, build sound projects, make certain their people are motivated, and work hard to achieve the strategies that the leader has set.

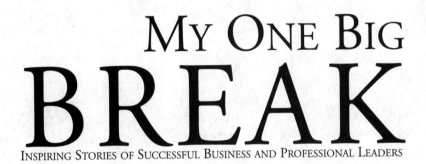

MY ONE BIG
BREAK

INSPIRING STORIES OF SUCCESSFUL BUSINESS AND PROFESSIONAL LEADERS

RAND V. ARASKOG

I had a lot of breaks in my business career, but the one that stands out the most resulted from something that took place far from home—in Vietnam.

Harold S. Geneen, after a legendary beginning, had led ITT into a quagmire of public and legal problems that severely tainted the image of the company. Competition to succeed Geneen had become intense. As one of many corporate line vice presidents in ITT, I was responsible for 10 companies in the Defense/Space Group. At the age of 40, I was also one of the youngest in the company.

As the leader of a group of businesses whose primary customer was the Department of Defense of the U.S. Government, I never let those ITT "problems" become an excuse for not competitively winning and holding business with our military customers. We did well in that market, to the great admiration of our board of directors, which included people like John McCone, former director of the CIA and the Atomic Energy Commission.

Then, early in 1972—just before the final Tet (North Vietnamese) Offensive that led the United States to reconsider its role in Vietnam and, ultimately, to pull out—I set out to that war-torn part of the world to determine the state of ITT's Federal Electric Corporation (FEC), one of the 10 companies in my

RAND ARASKOG was the chief executive of ITT Corporation from 1979 through 1998 and chairman from 1980 through 1998, capping a 32-year career with the company. A graduate of the U.S. Military Academy at West Point, Araskog worked in the office of the Secretary of Defense from 1954 through 1959 and was the director of marketing and planning for the Aeronautical Division of Honeywell, Inc., before joining ITT. Araskog and his wife, Jessie, are the parents of three children and have six grandchildren. They live in Palm Beach, Florida.

charge, and to bring back a full report to our board. We had approximately 1,500 people employed in South Vietnam, where they maintained the electronic communications being used by U.S. forces. The following excerpt from my book, *The ITT Wars*, records the trip:

> *What I saw in Vietnam was difficult to take, especially for a West Point graduate: officers' clubs for generals, officers' clubs for colonels, officers' clubs for majors and clubs for noncommissioned officers, generals keeping their wives in Thailand and commuting from the war on weekends. There was even an officers' club at the Saigon military airport with a whorehouse. Just go through the purple door, they said.*
>
> *Rats crawled through the best hotels and around the best restaurants in Saigon. It was hard to enter a hotel elevator without spotting a beautiful prostitute who had flown in from some part of the world to make quick money. The place was sick. Army trucks barreled down the road, driven by civilians who had stolen them within the previous few days. The only encouraging aspect of Vietnam was its children—the schoolchildren running in the streets to go to school, holding hands, laughing, wearing spotless white or blue clothing. They were the happy future of Vietnam, if only it could become free—which, of course, it did not.*
>
> *In order to inspect our facilities on a mountaintop at Vung Tau, we took a helicopter flown by pilots who acted as if they were under the influence of drugs. They almost killed us, clipping treetops with their propeller blades on takeoff and landing. Heavily armed, with machine guns pointing out of both sides, the helicopter flew at high and low altitudes, depending on the nature of the terrain and the locations of the enemy. But the biggest threat to our safety seemed to be right there in the cockpit.*
>
> *We spent a week in Vietnam, meeting with several general officers and expressing dissatisfaction with the evacuation plans*

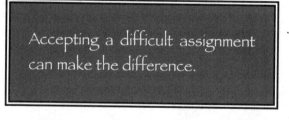

Accepting a difficult assignment can make the difference.

for the FEC employees there. We received assurances that those plans would be upgraded and that they would be implemented properly in the event that the expected Tet Offensive was successful.

My harrowing journey and the subsequent report I presented to Harold Geneen and to the board of ITT about our activities in Vietnam cast me onto center stage as "one who might ultimately be Geneen's successor."

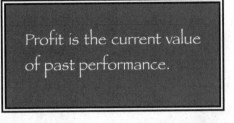

Profit is the current value of past performance.

Soon thereafter, another 12 companies headquartered in North America were added to my supervision. I was clearly on the way. A couple more breaks, not unusual in corporate histories, came along to ensure my eventual succession of Geneen—but I believe the catalyst was that foray into Southeast Asia during a period of such horrendous instability.

BOB BENNETT

Before I had the opportunity to help develop the Franklin Quest day planner, I had worked for many other businesses and in government positions. I will never forget my father's advice when I was preparing to leave for college and had not yet decided on a major. He told me it didn't matter what I majored in—what I was going to college for was to learn how to think, and he was exactly right.

I was working for a company called Microsonics in California in 1984 when a friend of mine called me from Salt Lake City. He told me he was starting a small company and asked me for some advice about their business plan.

My friend also asked me to come on board with them as the CEO. I was already working full-time as CEO of Microsonics, but they gave me their approval to run both companies at the same time.

The fledgling company had only four employees: my friend and his wife and two young associates. They did, however, have some big ideas. The company was going to hold business seminars about time management and sell a day planner that they had designed.

I advised them that they should not sell the day planner separately—they should give it away as part of the seminar. Then, if

BOB BENNETT was elected to a second term in the United States Senate in 1998. A Republican from Utah, Bennett is the son of four-term senator Wallace Bennett. He is the Chief Deputy Majority Whip of the Senate and is chairman of the Joint Economic Committee. A graduate of the University of Utah, Bennett worked in both private industry and in various positions in Washington before deciding to run for the Senate in 1992. He and his wife, Joyce, are the parents of six children.

people liked it and used it, they would reorder it for the next year. The company would be able to live off the reorders.

This was a somewhat risky proposition, but my friends listened to my advice and agreed to try it. We ordered 5,000 copies and began handing them out at the seminars.

People seemed to like the planners, but we knew we couldn't measure our level of success until it came time for the reorders at the end of the year. I knew if we could get 65 percent of the people to whom we had given the day planners to reorder them, we would have a business. If not, we would be finished.

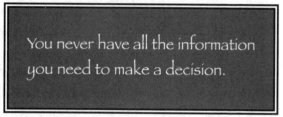

You never have all the information you need to make a decision.

That first year, we received renewal orders at a rate of 95 percent. The Franklin day planner had achieved success. In time, we were handing out 30,000 day planners a month.

As with every startup business, it was a tense time during those few months while we waited to find out if our idea would be profitable or not. People often sink all of their savings into a new business, and if it doesn't work, they can be financially ruined.

I recently heard Mitt Romney give a speech in which he said there are only two reasons why businesses fail—they run out of money, and they run out of money because they lose their focus.

One of the lessons we were able to draw from came from Mil Batten, who for years was the CEO and chairman of the board of J.C. Penney and later was the president of the New York Stock Exchange. I worked for him as Penney's first lobbyist in Washington from 1964-1968. His advice was always to focus on the customer, to do whatever you had to do to make sure the customer felt good about your company.

He gave the example of a customer coming in to return a shirt. When the clerk looked at the label, he saw the shirt had come from one of Penney's competitors. Mil posed this question: What should the employee do?

The correct response, of course, is to exchange the shirt. Now the clerk just has an inventory control problem, he said—somehow one of Penney's competitor's shirts had gotten into its inventory.

We tried to carry that philosophy with us as we built Franklin. Any time someone would stop me on the street and tell me they had a problem with the day planner, I would give them a new one for free. For years, our entire advertising campaign was based on word of mouth—that was all the advertising we needed.

I stayed as CEO of Franklin until 1992, when I decided to resign in order to follow my father and run for the U.S. Senate from Utah.

A political campaign operates exactly the same way as a business, especially a startup business. Many of the lessons I learned in the business world proved very valuable to me, not only on the campaign trail but also after I returned to Washington to begin my political career—the most important lesson being that you have to stay focused.

> Businesses fail because they lose their focus.

ROY BOSTOCK

During the spring of my senior year at Duke, I thought my future was pretty well determined. I was going to be graduating in a couple of months, and in June I was going to marry the woman I had been dating since high school. The following fall, I was going to begin law school at Duke while continuing to play football, having gained an extra year of eligibility and another tuition-free year because of a red-shirt season.

Then one evening came a knock on the door of my dorm room that changed my life.

When I opened the door, the man standing there introduced himself as Dean Rollins from the Harvard Business School. I had never met him and had never thought about the Harvard Business School. I knew about Harvard, having been accepted there as a undergraduate when I was coming out of high school, before accepting a football scholarship to Duke.

Dean Rollins explained to me that the Harvard Business School recruited top graduates from universities around the country. Through conversations with people at Duke, he had identified me as a candidate. I think I passed for what was considered diversity in 1962, being a football player from a Southern university who was an English literature major.

ROY BOSTOCK is chairman of the Partnership for a Drug-Free America, a not-for-profit organization based in New York City. Bostock also is the chairman of the Committee for Economic Development, a Washington, D.C.-based public policy group. He retired from a 38-year career in the advertising business in 2002, having served as the president of Benton & Bowles and as the chairman and CEO of D'Arcy Masius Benton & Bowles. In 1996 he created the MacManus Group, a global communications services company and in 2000 led the merger of that company with the Leo Burnett Co. to form B I Com^3, then the seventh largest global agency group. B I Com^3 was acquired by Publicis Groupe in Paris in 2002, creating the fourth largest global group. A graduate of Duke University, Bostock also is a graduate of the Harvard Business School. He lives in Rye, New York, with his wife, Merilee. They have three grown children.

He told me that as a graduate of the Harvard Business School, I would have many more alternatives available to me than I would after graduating from law school. My wife to be and I talked it over, and finally decided maybe he was right and we should give it a shot. I filled out the application, took the entrance exams and two months later received a letter saying I had been accepted and providing me the information on when I was to show up at Harvard. To this day I don't know what kind of scores I got on those tests.

I think back on those few months and realize how much the rest of my life was affected by that decision and by the two years I spent at the Harvard Business School. I showed up and thought I was terribly out of place. Everyone else it seemed had an engineering degree from MIT. They were all walking around with slide rules on their belts, and I didn't know a slide rule from a horse whip.

I stuck it out and enjoyed it, especially after taking a marketing class my first year. Near the end of the class, I asked the professor what he thought I should do for a summer job. He said since I loved marketing and with my background as an English major, I should look into the advertising agency business.

I didn't know advertising from a hole in the head, but I found out there were some agencies who were hiring summer interns. I applied at Benton & Bowles and was hired to work in their New York office. I loved the entire experience.

When I went back to Harvard, and it came time to look for a full-time job, Benton & Bowles invited me back and I quickly said yes and stayed there, or with the new companies they became part of, for my entire career.

I never would have ended up at an advertising agency if I had gone to law school. My life might have been just as interesting, but somehow I doubt it.

I loved the creative aspect of my job. I didn't really realize how much I loved that when I was at Duke. I liked working with creative people and coming up with new ideas. As soon as I got to Benton & Bowles, I knew that was where I wanted to be. I loved the phenomenon of sitting with people and looking at a problem and coming up with an idea that hadn't existed before.

Much of the success I had was with the introduction of new products, particularly for Procter & Gamble. I joined that account 12 months after going to work for Benton & Bowles, and basically stayed there for my entire career.

I was involved with the introduction and marketing of Scope, Dawn, Bounce, Charmin with the test marketing and national expansion of Pampers, the Rely tampon and Always sanitary napkin, and with Swiffer. We also had a good run building up the Hardee's brand name and expanding it out of the Southeast.

Moving up through the company, I became president of Benton & Bowles in 1984 and in 1990, became chairman and CEO of D'Arcy, Massius Benton & Bowles. We kept making acquisitions and building the company, and I became chairman and CEO of the newly formed McManus Group until 2000, when we merged that company with Leo Burnett in Chicago.

The company changed its name to B|Com^3, and I was chairman of that for about a year before retiring. B|Com^3 was acquired by Publicis S.A., and is now the fourth largest global communications company in the world.

I didn't stay retired for long, however, agreeing to become the chairman of the Partnership for a Drug Free America, succeeding Jim Burke in the pro-bono job. Our goal is to drive down the use of illicit drugs in the United States, and our marketing and advertising campaigns are working.

The secret to my success really is the same as most people—I found a job that I truly loved. People make a terrible mistake when they go into an endeavor just to make money. You have to find something you really enjoy that is suited to your talents. If you pursue that, it is going to lead to success.

A large part of a person's success depends on his or her ability to work effectively with other people. One of the keys for me was to have that strong liberal arts background before I went to the Harvard Business School. The importance of that broad-based background, before going into a particular specialty, is something I have emphasized for years.

Specialists don't become leaders. Generalists become leaders, usually because they have better skills at dealing with people.

EDWARD A. BRENNAN

My wife was in the hospital, having just given birth to our first son, when I accepted the job offer that would shape my entire career.

I had become interested in the retail business as a senior in high school when I began working for Benson-Rixon, a chain of eight men's apparel stores in Chicago and one in Milwaukee. I worked there through college at Marquette, then as an assistant buyer after graduation. Two years later I was promoted to buyer of basic men's apparel and accessories such as hosiery, belts, ties and cuff links, but I realized my future would be limited at such a small company.

So at age 22, I gave up a job at a small chain of men's clothing stores, took a 50-percent pay cut and moved from Chicago to become a trainee at the Sears store in Madison, Wisconsin.

I had interviewed with Sears when I was a senior in college and had been offered a position, but I turned it down. Two years later, I changed my mind and contacted them again. Luckily, I was given another offer.

It really was not a hard decision, despite taking the cut in pay from $10,000 a year—which in 1956 was a pretty good salary, especially for someone my age—to $4,800. The pay cut was a short-term problem, but the long term was far more important. I

EDWARD BRENNAN retired as chairman and CEO of Sears, Roebuck and Co. in 1995 after a 39-year career. He started with Sears in 1956 selling home furnishings at a store in Madison, Wisconsin, and rose through the ranks to become the 11th chairman of Sears in 1986. In 2003, he was elected executive chairman of AMR Corporation, the parent of American Airlines, but relinquished the title in 2004 and assumed the title of lead director. Brennan, a graduate of Marquette University, and his wife, Lois, have six children.

had decided I wanted my career to be in the retail business, and I felt I could become more successful in a big firm.

Sears insisted that all new employees start at the bottom of the corporate ladder; thus, the move to Madison. My clothing store experience, however, allowed me to move up rapidly through the company and pro-

"Just do the right thing" and others will follow your lead.

vided a competitive edge that I never lost throughout my career.

I know some people do not enjoy working in the retail industry, but I always found the job exciting, no matter what the assignment. It is a goal-oriented business and one in which it is very easy to track your performance, even on a daily basis.

I think the greatest impact on my career came from managing a full-line Sears store, which provided hands-on experience that proved invaluable in each successive position. What made the biggest impression on me was the recognition of superior performance by management. I enjoyed whatever job I had, and I always tried to do it to the best of my ability. I was never worried about what promotions might await me, convinced that would take care of itself.

I worked as the assistant store manager in Oshkosh, Wisconsin, and we had an outstanding period of sales and profit following several difficult years. The district executives recommended me for a promotion, and I was offered a job at the Chicago headquarters as an assistant buyer.

This new position exposed me to the corporate officers, and later I was offered a position on the staff of the vice president of marketing. He was a great mentor, and it was his encouragement that prompted me to go back to work in the stores, providing me with an even greater depth of experience.

I never was someone who was waiting for the phone to ring with another promotion or job offer. Our family moved many times while our children were growing up, and we always treated every new assignment as if we were going to stay there forever. We bought a house and cheered for the local teams—you couldn't cheer for the Bears after you had relocated to Boston.

When I was managing in Baltimore, the vice president for the east, Ed Telling, visited my store. The visit seemed to be low-key, but two weeks later he asked me to become the assistant general manager for the stores in metropolitan New York. My immediate boss there had serious health problems, which forced me to assume even more responsibility rather quickly. Telling later became the chairman and CEO of Sears, and he promoted me through a series of assignments, which ultimately culminated in my succeeding him upon his retirement.

During a 39-year career at Sears, I held 19 different positions, including assistant store manager, assistant buyer, store manager, district manager, executive vice president for a region, president and chief operating officer, and finally, chairman and chief executive officer. This included running some of Sears' more diversified companies, including Allstate, Dean Witter and Coldwell Banker.

I have often wondered what might have happened to my career if Telling's visit to my store in Baltimore had gone poorly, but I think one of the reasons it went well was that I wasn't expecting a future job to be riding on the outcome.

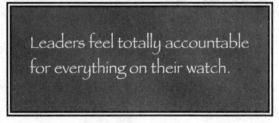

Leaders feel totally accountable for everything on their watch.

Another advantage I had in my career was that I never worked for a company or a boss who asked me to do anything that I felt ashamed to go home and tell my kids about. To me, that was always the acid test. Beyond doing the right thing, feeling completely accountable for anything that happens in a corporation is absolutely essential for a chairman or chief executive officer.

I still serve on five corporate boards, and I know the successful companies are ones where the executives live by the credo, "Just do the right thing." That attitude at the top of the ladder is one that permeates all the way down to the bottom and makes the entire corporation much stronger and a better place to work.

NANCY BRINKER

When I was young, I had a strong belief that I could make a difference in some way in my life. When I was five and my sister, Susan, was eight, our mother told us in a loving but very stern way that she expected us to be stewards of our country.

Our first experience in being "good stewards" came when my sister decided we should host an event to raise money in our neighborhood in Peoria, Illinois for polio victims. My sister told me to sing and dance and she would sell tickets for one dollar each. We asked all of the neighbors to come—and 64 people showed up. I thought I was wonderful, but after the show my sister very diplomatically told me that next time she would sing and dance and I would sell the tickets. I didn't know then that fundraising would become such a big part of my life.

I have had many mentors and teachers, among them my parents. My father at age 88 is a dedicated real estate executive who worked relentlessly to build a very good life for his family. My mother has always been focused on other people and involved in public service. I went to the University of Illinois—my father wanted me to go to law school, but I wanted to learn business and marketing.

I was able to get a job in the executive training program at Neiman Marcus. Stanley Marcus, founder of Neiman Marcus, was

NANCY GOODMAN BRINKER founded the Susan G. Komen Breast Cancer Foundation after the death of her sister, Suzy, who succumbed to the disease in 1980 at the age of 36. Currently the Komen Foundation boasts more than 75,000 volunteers working through a growing network of 112 U.S. and international affiliates. The recipient of many awards and honors, Ms. Brinker was appointed Ambassador to Hungary in 2001 by President Bush. She now lives in Palm Beach, Florida.

a wonderful mentor. He taught me so much, beginning with the fact that the customer is never wrong. Second, no means maybe, and third, most of selling is presentation, presentation, presentation. He also taught me to never give up, because the next time you might get the sale.

I stayed there for four and a half years, and I loved fashion but I didn't like selling clothes. I really wanted to find a higher purpose in my life. I met and married Norman Brinker, who built a successful restaurant business, including Steak and Ale and Chili's. Norman built his company with several key principles, including to always have a vision, to share your vision and to get people to buy into your dream.

Norman always said you don't ask people to come to work for a job, but to join the dream and create a team, give them responsibility, and if you don't care who gets the credit, you will be amazed at what you can get done. He also said you had to allow people to fail occasionally, because that was the only way they could learn, and then would work even harder to have success. His work ethic was always to work like it is play, and to play like hell.

Little did I know that all of his advice, and my desire to find a higher purpose in my life, were going to come together out of tragedy. My sister died from breast cancer in 1981, and I found the core meaning of my life by starting the Susan G. Komen Breast Cancer Foundation.

What amazed me was that we had made such a national issue out of all the men and women who were killed during the Vietnam War—59,000 Americans—yet I found out that during the same length of time 339,000 women died from breast cancer, and nobody was holding rallies or protests about that.

I knew we had to change the culture of our society. We had to make people aware of how serious the problem was, and I knew we had to make it big to accomplish what we wanted to get done. It had to be a cause that was on everyone's lips. It was my desire to help other women and their families so they wouldn't have to suffer the way my sister and our family did.

I am tremendously moved by how successful the Foundation has become.

I was also fortunate enough to also honor my mother's goal to be a "good steward" by accepting President Bush's request to become the U.S. Ambassador to Hungary in 2000. I specifically asked for Hungary. Five years earlier, in 1995, I had visited Prague in the Czech Republic while my son was attending college there for a year. We went to a memorial chapel, and the name of my mother's cousin literally jumped out at me from the wall on which it was written. Seeing firsthand a relative's name on a memorial greatly affected me—I was reminded of the atrocities our family had endured during World War II. I thought the position in Hungary would take me to that same part of the world, where I hoped I could make a difference.

One area in our country that still needs help is the discrimination toward women, especially in the corporate world. You have to work extremely hard to become a successful woman. A lot of men my age and older are still not comfortable with a woman being in a position of authority.

The problem this creates for women is that it often keeps them from reaching their full potential, and, just like men, many women are not happy unless they are productive. They are forced to search for an alternative path, and sometimes they just can't get where they really want to get.

My message to all women, however, is to keep going. In the quest for your cause, be brave and remember that "no" only means "maybe." There is hope and the world is changing. There always will be room for improvement, but the only way it will get better is by making people realize that it has to get better.

That was what we did with the Susan G. Komen Breast Cancer Foundation. We were able to change the culture, and now people realize just how serious the problem is, and much work is being done to try to find a cure for this terrible disease.

My father sent me a quote once from the author Lorraine Hansberry that depicts my thoughts on being successful. "The thing that makes you exceptional, if you are at all, is inevitably that which must make you lonely."

JOHN W. BROWN

By the fall of 1965, I had grown tired of working in the defense industry. One of the little-known facts that they don't tell you about until it's too late is the people there spend only about half of their time working on the project they are assigned to—the other half they're making a pitch for the next big project.

I wanted to do something else.

Before moving into the defense industry, I had worked for the Olin Corp. At that time, they told me that if, somewhere down the line, I was ever looking for a new job to be sure and call. So I did just that, and that led to a job offer from Ernest Johnson, the president of E.R. Squibb & Sons, which was owned by Olin.

Frankly, there were few compelling reasons for Ernie to hire me. Nevertheless, he did, and I went to work for a man who became the biggest influence on me during the remainder of my professional career.

Ernie had a simple philosophy of life: Battles are to be won; defeat or compromise is unthinkable. He was a former marine lieutenant and had fought in the Pacific during World War II. (Interestingly, as both a pharmaceutical executive and a devout Christian Scientist, he never, to my knowledge, took any medicine—not even an aspirin or a teaspoon of cough syrup.) Although he did not wear his faith on his sleeve, his faith in the Almighty

JOHN W. BROWN began his career as an engineer for the Ormet Corp., an aluminum manufacturer, after graduating from Auburn University. After working for Thiokol Chemical Corp., Brown joined Squibb Corp. in 1965. He served in a variety of positions before he became president of Edward Weck & Co., a Squibb subsidiary, in 1972. Brown held that position until 1977, when he became president and CEO of Stryker Corp., in Kalamazoo, Michigan. Brown was appointed chairman of the board in 1980. He is married and the father of two grown daughters.

was unshakable. He was fearless and expected the same of his leaders.

Ernie believed a good manager could handle any situation and that a capable leader could bring out the best in people no matter what the circumstances. Accepting Ernie's job offer was an immediate enrollment in "Ernie Johnson's On the Job MBA Program." It was one of the most grueling management development programs you could imagine.

It was sink or swim.

There were no mentors, no classes, no understudy jobs. You were given the job, and if you failed, you were never consulted or spoken to again. If you succeeded, then you received another assignment—but always before you had completely mastered your current job.

During my first five years at Squibb, I moved through a variety of jobs—new product coordinator, manufacturing manager, project manager, personnel director, and assistant to the president. It was a tremendous learning experience, and one of the most important lessons I learned was how vital it is to be completely honest and to adhere to your financial numbers. We didn't have a lot of new products, and yet Ernie wanted to see growth every year. He was very good at measuring the marketplace and controlling costs.

In 1971, Squibb acquired Edward Weck & Co., a manufacturer of manual surgical instruments for general, ENT and ophthalmic surgery. My job was to make certain this new division was successful, adopting Squibb's rigorous accounting and operating procedures while meeting all financial goals. It was made very clear I would be fully accountable if anything went wrong.

At the time of the acquisition, Weck's president was less than a year away from retirement. He said he would stay through an orderly integration, then retire. Ernie asked me to prepare a list of potential successors, so I gave him a list of four well qualified candidates.

None of the four made the cut.

One was considered too valuable in his current job. Another turned the job down. Ernie didn't think a third candidate was that well qualified, and the fourth left the company. In frustration, Ernie turned to me and asked, "Do you think you can do the job?"

I was caught off guard, but I managed to stammer a "yes" response.

I never did find out whether he had actually intended to offer me the job, or whether it was simply a stroke of luck for me that had come from his exasperation.

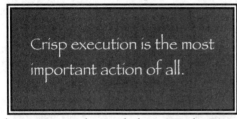

Crisp execution is the most important action of all.

It was a pretty heady job for a 37-year-old without an Ivy League degree. Ernie retired a few months later, and the Squibb bureaucracy descended on Weck. Fortunately, our numbers were good. I remained president of Weck for five years, during which time our sales doubled and our profits tripled.

I didn't really realize it as it was happening, but Ernie had moved me through a variety of business units, including research, manufacturing, marketing, sales and distribution. He had prepared me well for the challenges that awaited me, including becoming the president and CEO of Stryker Corporation in 1977.

Over the past 28 years, Stryker has grown from a $17 million private business to a $4.3 billion medical device company with 16,000 employees, listed on the New York Stock Exchange. Early on, investment bankers told us that if we wanted to be seen as a growth company, we had to grow our earnings by 20 percent a year. We have done it all but one year, when we took a hit for an acquisition.

What we have learned is that a goal is critical to success and a plan is important, but execution is the most important thing of all. We spend maybe 15 percent of our time on planning and 85 percent on execution. I think where many companies mess up is that they spend too much time on strategy and not nearly enough time on execution. The beauty of our process is that we don't argue about our goal for the budget; we just know we have to go all out to hit it. And following Ernie's philosophy, anything less is unacceptable.

JAMES E. BURKE

My first "job" involved selling items door to door or from a small roadside stand in my hometown outside Albany, New York, so I learned early on the importance of being able to market my product if I wanted to be a successful salesman. Later, in the mid 1950s, after graduating from Princeton and the Harvard Business School, followed by a stint in the navy and a short period working for Procter & Gamble, I went to work for Johnson & Johnson.

After about a year, I was summoned to the office of George Smith, the president of the company. I believed at that time that Johnson & Johnson was not as aggressive in the consumer marketing area as I thought the company should be, and I was wondering if I would be better off looking for a job with a different company. Mr. Smith apparently had heard of my dissatisfaction, and that was why he wanted to talk to me.

He asked me about my opinions, and we discussed the poor performance of the company in the consumer markets and the almost total absence of vital new products. The meeting culminated in Mr. Smith asking me if I would like to start a new products effort at Johnson & Johnson within the consumer products division.

JAMES E. BURKE is the former chairman of the board and CEO of Johnson & Johnson. He headed the company from 1976 until his retirement in 1989. Burke joined Johnson & Johnson as a product director in 1953 and served the company in various capacities before his appointment as chairman and CEO. Burke is currently the chairman emeritus of the board of the Partnership for a Drug-Free America, an organization he headed following his retirement from Johnson & Johnson. He has also served on the boards of numerous charities, and in 2000 was presented with the Presidential Medal of Freedom by president Bill Clinton. A graduate of Holy Cross College, Burke earned his MBA at Harvard Business School. He and his wife, Didi, are the parents of two children.

My answer was a very enthusiastic yes, and I went to work diligently on my new assignment. Over the next year, I took on two new products that had already undergone the testing phase and looked as if they had a reasonable chance of success.

Both products failed.

I was very disappointed—and not surprised when I was told General Johnson, the very active and decisive chairman of the corporation, had sent word for me to report to his office.

I was certain I was going to be fired, and justifiably so. I had been given an assignment and it had not gone well.

General Johnson had a huge office, and I felt properly diminished as I walked from the door to his desk. He was sitting with his back to me. I was even more convinced that I was about to be fired.

When General Johnson turned around, I saw he was holding a piece of paper. On it was the data about the two products I had been assigned to develop, about how they had failed and the cost to the corporation. He asked for validation of the numbers, and I sadly confirmed them.

With that, General Johnson stood up, stuck out his right hand and said, "Thank you for your courage in introducing these new products. Taking risk is at the very heart of building new businesses. We need more of this in our consumer divisions, or for that matter, in all of our businesses."

This obviously turned out to be the biggest break of my career.

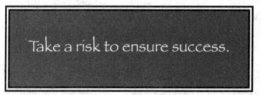

Take a risk to ensure success.

I was shocked, but very pleasantly surprised. We then turned the focus of our meeting to other products that were in various stages of development. I gave him my honest opinions about them, giving him the reasons why I was optimistic they would be successful. Fortunately, many of those products did turn out to be profitable.

General Johnson firmly believed the philosophy, which he developed in 1943, that you have to take risks in order to make a success of the new products you believe in. This became Johnson & Johnson's credo, and it has stood the test of time.

Personally, I was captivated by it. During my period as chairman and CEO of the company, I was determined to ensure that this philosophy remained healthy and strong. I started having "challenge" meetings—employees would come in and read the credo, and then I would try to create arguments against it, making them prove to me that it was still valid. This led to a better understanding of it and to a greater appreciation of it by everyone. I think this concept helped to produce more positive results for the company.

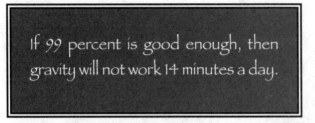

If 99 percent is good enough, then gravity will not work 14 minutes a day.

At no point in the company's history was our philosophy challenged more than it was during the Tylenol crisis of 1982, when the McNeil Consumer & Specialty Pharmaceuticals product was adulterated with cyanide and used as a murder weapon. With Johnson & Johnson's good name and reputation at stake, I know there were many times when all of the executives relied heavily on the philosophy embodied in the credo. Luckily the crisis passed and the company's reputation was preserved.

JOHN CAPSTICK

I began my career in England at 20 years of age. The experience I gained during my career by working in the United States and for U.S.-based companies, however, definitely was a factor in my success. I learned that Americans definitely work a lot harder than Europeans. They work longer hours, take shorter lunch breaks and have much less time off. Most workers in Germany get six weeks of vacation a year—that's unheard of in the United States. I think that harder work ethic is part of the reason for our productivity.

Once I had completed my compulsory two years of military service, I decided to join the printing industry as a management trainee. In 1971, I was hired by one of England's largest privately held printing companies in York, England. The chairman and principal shareholder was a charismatic, somewhat eccentric character—Bernard Johnson. He was a multilingual academic and would have been much more at home as master of one of Cambridge Colleges than running a printing company.

I worked for him for four years, eventually becoming the managing director of the company. He unfortunately became ill and put me in charge of the company, giving me a 10 percent share. Two days before he died, we had an emergency board meeting in his hospital room and he appointed me chairman. He did-

JOHN A. CAPSTICK spent 35 years working in the international printing industry. He was a group president of R.R. Donnelley & Sons Co., the world's largest commercial printing company, which employs more than 34,000 people in 150 locations around the world. Capstick joined Ben Johnson & Co., one of England's largest privately controlled printers, in 1970 and became chairman and CEO in 1973. He sold the company to R.R. Donnelley in 1978 and helped Donnelley greatly expand its international business before retiring from the company in 1994. He is married and the father of two sons and currently resides in Surrey, England.

n't have any immediate family other than his wife, and she was not involved in the business.

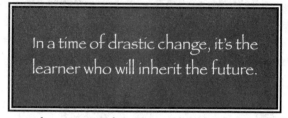

In a time of drastic change, it's the learner who will inherit the future.

The three controlling shareholders, Bernard's widow, Hansi, and two lady cousins, left me to run the growing business. About two years after Bernard's death, Hansi told me she would like to sell her majority interest in the company and move closer to her family in Switzerland.

Having since gained much experience and knowledge from selling several companies, today I would opt for a leveraged buy-out. Being too busy at that time, however, with the day-to-day operations of the company and without such experience, I decided to reach for the stars and approached the Chicago-based R.R. Donnelley Co., which was the world's largest printing company, to see if they might be interested in buying our company.

It was very much a long shot, for several reasons.

In 1978, Donnelley was featured in *Guinness Book of World Records* as the world's largest printer, but still it was a very conservative company. They did not even have any operations west of the Rockies in the United States—still viewing it as the Wild West—much less printing plants and facilities in foreign countries. Furthermore, the company was non-union and committed to remaining that way. Our company in England was a union shop.

Still, I wanted to make the effort.

I arranged to meet Jim Donnelley for dinner, and he listened to my story. The next day he introduced me to Gaylord Donnelley, the company's patriarch, and Chuck Lake, the company's brilliant chairman and CEO.

It was a very ambitious decision for them, but they decided to buy our company. I was named a senior vice president and the first overseas officer. For two years, we continued to grow, and I think both sides were pleased with how the operations were going.

None of us knew, however, that the company was about to experience a major change.

When Margaret Thatcher became prime minister, she began to sell all of the government-owned businesses. Thatcher was determined to break the grip of the trade unions that had brought Britain to its knees. She started with the largest union concentration in the infrastructure companies such as coal, transportation and telecommunications, which controlled massive pieces of England's economy. British Rail, for example, owned a large number of hotels plus the cross-channel ferries. Thatcher's plan was to break up these monopolies and privatize the residual pieces.

British Telecom was then part of the post office and printed its own telephone directories in two inefficient, overmanned, government-owned printing plants. As part of Thatcher's plan, the government closed the yellow pages plant at Harrow, near London, and put out a tender for a 10-year contract to print all of the yellow pages directories in Britain.

My plant in York had never printed directories, but Donnelley was the world leader in that category with many plants in the United States. I took the CEO of Yellow Pages, plus the responsible government officer, with me and we flew to the directory plants in the United States on one of Donnelley's private jets. The magic worked, and we were awarded the contract.

We built a new plant with state-of-the-art equipment—including the first robots in the history of the British printing industry. The product was a great success, and British Telecom asked us to take over a second plant in Northern England. When the plant was updated and ready, we received the contract to print all of the White Pages directories in Britain.

That contract also was for 10 years, and the value of the two combined contracts was more than $1 billion. Suddenly, British Telecom, not Sears or Time Warner, was Donnelley's largest customer.

A new group, the International Group, was formed and I became group president. The company was so thrilled with our success that they identified more potential markets in other countries, and we were able to expand Donnelley's reach across Europe and into Southeast Asia. Donnelley truly became an international company, and today it remains the largest printer in the world.

RICHARD E. CAVANAGH

My big break came when, as a freshman, I stepped onto the campus of Wesleyan University.

I really had no idea what career I wanted to pursue as a youngster growing up in Metuchen, New Jersey, where my dad was a mid-level civil servant, working as a supply officer for a Veterans Hospital. My mom stayed home to take care of my brother, who was handicapped.

Waking up at four o'clock in the morning when I was 13 years old to go door to door delivering milk was not my idea of fun. Three days a week, though, I would drag myself out of bed to meet the driver of the milk truck at 4:30 a.m. so I could complete my route before going to school.

That job didn't last long, and neither did my stints as paper-boy, cabana boy, office boy, clerk at a refinery or porter in a box factory. As I tried my hand at this job or that, I knew that I didn't want to do any of them. They all required hard work, and I am basically lazy.

It was at Wesleyan that I made a wonderful and welcome real-ization. There I learned that plenty of jobs were available that weren't so physically demanding, jobs that didn't require me to get up so early in the morning.

RICHARD CAVANAGH is president and chief executive officer of The Conference Board, Inc., a global research and business membership group. The Conference Board connects more than 2,500 enterprises in 60 countries and is the most widely cited private source of business intelligence. Cavanagh joined The Conference Board in 1995 after serving as executive director of the John F. Kennedy School of Government at Harvard University for eight years. He previously worked for McKinsey & Company, Inc., and for the White House Office of Management and Budget under President Carter.

Over the years since leaving Wesleyan, I have held several different jobs, and the one key component of all of them was that they were fun. If I had not liked what I was doing, I know I would not have been as successful.

My first "real job" was working as a bookkeeper for Johnson & Johnson in the summer before I began pursuing a graduate degree at the Harvard Business School. After earning my degree, I went to work for McKinsey & Company, a management consulting firm. I spent 17 years with the company and led the firm's public issues consulting practices, working with many Fortune 500 companies, emerging enterprises, governments and nonprofit organizations along the way.

During those years, I learned well the advice that my father had given me about the importance of having good friends. Many of the lucky breaks that have come my way during my career can be attributed to the fact that I had people looking out for me.

In 1976, several of these friends were working on the Jimmy Carter presidential campaign, and since they knew I was poor enough to be a Democrat, they asked me to help develop some promises for the campaign. One of my key jobs at McKinsey had been reorganizing companies, so I drew from that experience and made promises about reorganizing the government.

As it turned out, Carter was elected president, and we had to figure out how to keep the promises we had made.

I took a leave of absence from McKinsey in order to work on the presidential transition team, and then accepted a job working in the Office of Management and Budget at the White House. I learned there that the government had become very good at accounting for money, but they weren't very good about doing things like depositing it. The government was missing out on a lot of interest, so we came up with a plan to improve cash management that saved the government about $12 billion.

Because I had been able to help save that money, they gave me a new job—figuring out how to spend it. It may sound strange, but this job was much harder. I was able to help direct the president's reorganization project for domestic programs, though, which really improved the management of various governmental agencies.

Working at the White House was great fun, but after two years I decided to return to McKinsey, where Marvin Bower, a co-founder of the firm, took me under his wing. Eight years later I received another offer I couldn't refuse—the position of executive dean of the John F. Kennedy School of Government at Harvard, which also came my way through a friend.

I enjoyed that job as well, before I left eight years later to assume my current job as the president and chief executive officer of The Conference Board, a global research and business member-ship organization that has more than 2,500 members in 60 countries. Its mission is to improve the business enterprise system and to enhance the contributions of business to society.

Through all of my various positions, I realize how lucky I have been. I learned about business at McKinsey; I learned about research at Harvard; and at both of those jobs and at the White House I learned about aspiring to be the best.

I never had a strategic plan for my career, and I'm glad I didn't. One of the biggest lessons I have learned is that it doesn't matter where you start your career or what job you have. What is important is that you do that job very well, because that is what gets people to notice you. I think too many people tend to overemphasize a rigid plan. They'll say something like, "By next year I want to be the assistant product manager or a vice president or whatever." Or they'll think, "I ought to be making this amount of money."

> It's important to have good friends—they make you lucky.

I think those folks are the ones who are most often disappointed, because most careers don't work out like that. That is why it is so important to get a job that you like, and one at which you can succeed, rather than making a master plan. It's also important to realize there's a lot of work involved—and that good friends make you lucky.

GEORGE A. COHON

When I was about 12 years old, I began working in my grandfather's plumbing fixtures store on the south side of Chicago. My job was to count how many nuts and bolts were in each bin. During school I continued to work a variety of jobs—I worked construction, I sold shoes, I was a tree trimmer for the city of Chicago.

After graduating from law school, I joined the firm owned by my father and brother-in-law. But I don't know that I intended to be a lawyer all my life.

One night in the spring of 1966, my wife, Susan, and I were pushing our oldest son, Craig, around the block in his stroller. We ran into a neighbor who knew that I was a lawyer, and he mentioned to me that he was interested in acquiring a McDonald's franchise, preferably in Hawaii.

I was always on the lookout for new clients, and asked if I could represent him. He agreed, and on his behalf, I began negotiations with Ray Kroc.

Kroc had bought out the original McDonald brothers in 1961, and two years later, the eight-restaurant chain had expanded to 550 restaurants across the United States. By 1966, McDonald's was selling hamburgers at the rate of one million a day.

GEORGE COHON is the founder and senior chairman of McDonald's Restaurants of Canada, Limited, and founder and chairman of McDonald's in Russia. A native of Chicago, Cohon graduated from Drake University and Northwestern University School of Law. Cohon practiced corporate law in Chicago from 1961 to 1967, when he moved to Toronto to become the licensee of McDonald's Corporation for Eastern Canada. He also founded Ronald McDonald House Charities in both Canada and Russia and is involved in many other charitable activities. He lives in Toronto with his wife, Susan. They have two sons.

Over nearly a year, I met with Kroc several times to discuss the Hawaii franchise. I was pretty sure the deal was going to go through. I liked Ray, he seemed to like me, and we were developing a good relationship.

As I quickly learned, however, Ray operated a lot on instinct, and his business instincts were very good. Despite our ongoing negotiations, Ray had gotten into a conversation with someone on an airplane—a bright, energetic business-

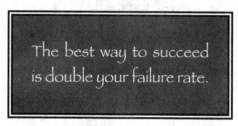

The best way to succeed is double your failure rate.

man who happened to live in Honolulu. By the time the plane had landed, my client's hopes of getting the Hawaii franchise were gone.

Ray called to break the news and offered an alternative, "The rights to most of eastern Canada are open."

Eastern Canada isn't exactly Hawaii, but I told Ray I would bring the offer to my client. When my client said he wasn't interested, I phoned Ray with his decision. I wasn't prepared for Ray's response.

"George," he said, "you don't want to be a lawyer for the rest of your life—why don't you get involved?"

I don't know how he knew it, but he was right. I didn't enjoy being a lawyer. I was frustrated. I found it tedious and boring. I hated keeping time records. I have nothing against lawyers; it just wasn't the job for me.

Still, it was more than a little risky to accept Ray's offer. It would mean moving my wife and two very young children to a foreign country where we knew no one. I had a lot of doubts—you have to admit your fear and trepidation if you are completely honest with yourself.

Susan and I sat up late into the night, discussing the possibility. She has never been afraid of risk or adventure, and the more we talked, the more excited we became. Despite our anxieties, I had a belief in Ray Kroc and McDonald's. So I said yes.

We opened the first McDonald's in eastern Canada in London, Ontario in 1968. I did everything at first, but I quickly found out I was better off standing on the other side of the counter talking to the customers than working back in the kitchen. We had some really good people who knew how to make hamburgers, and I knew how to clean the tables.

The restaurant did great, but we were so heavily in debt that we were constantly losing money until we got many more open. In 1972 we opened the first McDonald's in Montreal and continued to grow and expand.

By the time the Olympics came to Montreal in 1976, we were doing very well. We had a luxury bus that we used for charities, and the Canadian government called and asked if they could borrow the bus for the Olympics. The Soviet Union, which was going to host the Games in 1980, was sending a delegation to Montreal, and our government wanted to use the bus to transport them.

I was at the Games with my wife and two young children, wearing a T-shirt and jeans, when I saw the bus pull up and all of these dour-looking Russians get off. I said to Sue, "Let's go meet them."

We were stopped by the Mounted Police and the KGB. My business card is shaped like a hamburger (it's even an invitation for a free Big Mac). I handed my card to the security officer and said I would like to meet these people. One man stepped up, and it turned out he was with the Canadian government.

"I'm from the protocol department," he told me, "and these people are important visitors. You will have to go through the department of Foreign Affairs and Protocol to even get close to them."

I replied, "Well, my protocol is I own the bus."

That started the whole odyssey of bringing McDonald's to the Soviet Union. It took a dozen years of negotiations before we finally signed the contract allowing us to open a restaurant in Moscow. At the time, we were dealing with what president Ronald Reagan called the "evil empire," and the biggest challenge was working around the conflict between Adam Smith's free enterprise and Karl Marx's communism.

I never wanted to give up the fight, though, because I saw a country of 200 million people who were hungry. It was too important an opportunity to let it get away.

Since the opening of our first restaurant in Pushkin Square in Moscow in 1990, we have grown to 116 restaurants in 31 cities in Russia, employing more than 15,000 Russian citizens and proudly serving about 320,000 customers per day.

The Pushkin Square restaurant, which on its opening day served 30,000 people, has 27 cash registers and seating for 900 people. Pushkin still remains the busiest restaurant in the McDonald's system and will serve the 100th million customer during its 15-year anniversary in 2005.

I even wrote a book about the whole Russian experience, called *To Russia with Fries*, with the foreword written by former Russian Premier Mikhail Gorbachev.

What would my life have been like had Susan and I pushed our son's stroller in a different direction that night in 1966? I have no idea.

It was a really fortuitous meeting for me. If I had never had the chance to meet Ray Kroc and become involved with McDonald's, I very well might have continued to practice law.

I saw a sign in an office in Florida not too long ago that I thought was pretty prophetic—"It's what you learn after you know it all that counts."

What all of my dealings with McDonald's have taught me is persistence. I tell people not to get depressed when something doesn't go their way the first time. If you don't immediately get the job you want, don't let it get you down or stop you. If you work in a car wash, just think that maybe one day you will own the car wash.

That's the kind of attitude you have to have in order to succeed.

FRANK W. CONSIDINE

When I came back to Chicago after serving in the navy in World War II, I resumed working in the entertainment business, booking orchestras and bands and producing shows. I had done that while attending Loyola University, while also working at a golf course as a caddie and later as a starter.

I really enjoyed the entertainment business. It was fun at that age, and I think I would have stayed in the business for a while, but I don't know if I would have enjoyed making it my lifelong career. I had majored in philosophy at Loyola, intending to go to law school, but when I got back from the navy I didn't really want to start all over again in school.

I had been back about a year and a half when a friend from the Music Corporation of America and I were having lunch one day at the London House. A gentleman named Gerald Graham approached our table. I had known him because he played golf at the South Shore Country Club, where I had worked before the war.

It had been about five years since I had seen him, but he came up to me as if we were long-lost friends. "Where have you been?" he asked me.

Mr. Graham reminded me that he had told me to come see him when I got out of the navy. I thought he was saying that just

FRANK W. CONSIDINE is the retired chairman, president and chief executive officer of American National Can Company. He was elected president of the predecessor company, National Can Corporation, in 1969 and chief executive officer in 1975. He was chairman of the board from 1983 through 1990. A graduate of Loyola University in Chicago, Considine is involved in many charitable activities in Chicago and serves as the chairman of the board of Loyola University Health System. Considine and his wife, Nancy, are the parents of seven daughters and two sons.

to be nice, but it turned out he meant it. His office was in the same building as the restaurant, so after lunch I went up to his office.

Mr. Graham was the president of a glass container manufacturing company, and after a few meetings, he hired me as his assistant. I took a pay cut from the job I had in the entertainment business, accepting a salary of $6,000 a year plus expenses. I was 26 years old, single, and I really thought the job offered me a better career opportunity.

Mr. Graham gave me a great education in the glass manufacturing business, spending an hour or so with me almost every day to go over what had happened that day and what was planned for the next day. The lessons I learned there were invaluable to me for the rest of my career.

A few years later, after I had moved on to another glass manufacturer in Chicago, I received an offer to take over a small glass manufacturer in Minneapolis. It was a young company, and I really thought it had potential. Plus, I would own a majority of it with some other investors, so I took the challenge and accepted the job.

The operations were going fine and we had been manufacturing product for about a year when American Can Co., a much larger corporation, built a new plant in Minneapolis and hired away many of our key people. I couldn't blame them for leaving us, because American offered much higher wages and better benefits. There was no room for two plants and we couldn't compete, so we ended up liquidating the company.

It was a scary time. I had knowledge of the industry and was looking for another job when a second chance meeting redirected the course of my professional life.

My doctor, Dr. Charles Thompson, was also the personal physician for R.S. Solinksy, the chairman and CEO of National Can Corp. A friend of mine happened to bump into Dr. Thompson one day on Michigan Avenue and told him what was happening with our company. Dr. Thompson insisted on setting up a meeting for me with Mr. Solinksy. After a few meetings, I was hired as the vice president and general sales manager of National Can Co. I stayed there almost 40 years. In 1953, I became the president of the company. I went on to serve as chairman and CEO until I retired in 1988.

At the time, National Can was the third-ranked business in the industry with 14 plants and $100 million in revenue. Over time we built the company into the top-ranked business with 120 factories around the world and revenue of $4.5 billion.

We also purchased the American Can Co. and became American National Can, in effect allowing me to take over the company that had forced our small Minneapolis company out of business years before.

One of the keys to our success was that we became the first company to market an "easy-opening" beverage can, which had been developed by Alcoa. It took us only two days to decide to use their can top, because we were worried that they might take their offer to some other manufacturer if we didn't act quickly.

Until our competitors had time to catch up, we were overwhelmed with demand for the new can. American and Continental were slow to adopt the new design because their research departments were working on ideas of their own.

Quick decisions are always important to the success of any business. If your company allows a decision to get tangled up in its own bureaucracy, that will open the door for another company to run away with the idea. Being able to capitalize on the opportunities that present themselves to you makes all the difference between success and failure.

I have always thought that another major component to success in business is integrity. I have also looked to hire young people who have drive, creativity, good judgment and excellent interpersonal skills. There is a lot a person with all of those qualities can accomplish.

As my career has proved, however, it also doesn't hurt to have good luck and good friends watching out for you.

Integrity is the major component of winning companies.

J. MICHAEL COOK

My accounting career got off to a rather rocky beginning. When I was 12 years old, I got my first job, delivering the *Miami Daily News* every day after school in my hometown of Miami, Florida. The newspaper gave its delivery boys the papers, then settled up with them at the end of the month when they had collected the payments from their customers.

What I didn't realize as I collected the money from my customers, however, was that the cost of a monthly subscription was different than four times the weekly rate. I undercharged my customers and found myself short when it came time to pay the newspaper. I had to borrow the money from my mother to make up the difference.

Maybe it was that inauspicious beginning that drove me to become an accountant, but the source of my career is more likely traced to my counselor at the University of Florida, where I went not really having any idea what I wanted to study or what kind of career I wanted to pursue.

I had always enjoyed math, so I thought about majoring in that, but quickly found out that degree would only be good if I wanted to teach that subject or pursue a doctorate degree, and neither one of those possibilities excited me a great deal. That was when my counselor asked, "Have you thought about accounting?"

MIKE COOK is the retired chairman and CEO of Deloitte & Touche LLP, one of the country's leading professional services firms. He was also chairman of the Deloitte & Touche Foundation. Cook directed the global merger of Deloitte Haskins & Sekks and Touche Ross in 1989. He is active on many boards of directors and charitable organizations. A graduate of the University of Florida, Cook and his wife have three children and three grandchildren. They live in Greenwich, Connecticut.

The honest answer was no, but I took the chance and enrolled in the business school. It turned out to be the right decision.

When it came time to leave school and find a job, I also was very fortunate. I wanted to stay in south Florida and was able to get a job in Fort Lauderdale with one of the two major accounting firms in the state, Haskins & Sells, in a small office with only 15 employees. After a move to our Miami office, I was assigned to one of our newest clients, a company called the Delta Corporation of America, in part because the company's chief financial officer had been a classmate of mine at Florida.

This company was in a booming business in the late 1960s. They did mobile home financing, including everything from handling the credit to placing the insurance. The company turned out to have the fastest growth in one year of any company on the stock exchange.

Unfortunately, the next year it experienced the sharpest decline of any company on the stock exchange. What people had found out was that the mobile homes rapidly lost their value, so even though they had invested through a long-term sales contract, it was cheaper to walk away from the deal and buy a new mobile home. This left the company with a lot of uncollected loans, fees to be rebated and serious financial problems.

My firm sent a very senior partner down from the New York headquarters to investigate the situation, and he became a mentor and one of my biggest supporters. Our firm was sued by a lot of people who had lost a lot of money, but it was proven that we had not done anything wrong—to the contrary, we were credited with uncovering the problems. Potential adversity had become my one big break.

This partner was instrumental in recommending me for a position in the firm's national office in New York. Even though my wife and I did not want to leave South Florida, we knew it was an opportunity we could not turn down. I really valued the role all of my mentors had played in my career, and I trusted their advice and opinions.

I ended up working in the national office for eight years before returning to Miami. I was only there for a couple of years, however, before I was asked to return to New York as the managing partner of the firm, then known as Deloitte, Haskins & Sells. I ended up spending 15 years as the chairman and CEO of the company, retiring in 1999, after leading the company into the merger that created Deloitte & Touche.

When I retired, Deloitte & Touche was ranked eighth on the *Fortune* list of the 100 best companies to work for in America. We had more than 2,000 partners and 30,000 people working in the United States, and 5,000 partners and 60,000 people working in offices around the world. Our revenues exceeded $5 billion in the U.S. and $10 billion around the world.

One aspect of our business that I was particularly proud of was our ability to attract, retain and advance high-talent women, a big factor in our *Fortune* ranking. We had only the female partner when I became a partner in 1974, and now the number is approaching 600, 20 percent of the partnerships, and growing. What we found out is that women are attracted to accounting for much the same reasons as I was attracted to the business, and they are great professionals.

I never dreamed of becoming the CEO of our firm and certainly didn't plan for that outcome. Keys to my success were the mentors who took a personal interest in me. I listened to them and trusted in them and their judgment. If they asked me to do something, I believed it was the right thing for me to do because they knew more than I did. They were kind to me and put me in a position where I was able to show what I could do.

People in leadership positions in business today tend to forget sometimes that the best decisions you can make involve common sense. My approach to our business was always simply "happy clients, happy people," meaning that if we were doing our job well for our clients and our people, they would prosper and that would take care of all other aspects of the business. It really was not that complicated.

I don't think it requires spectacular vision to be successful in business, but it helps if you have the ability to see the obvious shortly before somebody else sees it.

ROBERT L. CRANDALL

Like so many vocational choices, my venture into the airline industry was a function of luck and accident. When I was working for Hallmark Cards in Kansas City, I had a neighbor who worked for TWA. His daughters would occasionally baby-sit for us—when they weren't jetting off to Rome or Paris for lunch or dinner.

One day TWA called and offered me a job, which I initially turned down. My wife kept after me—asking, "Wouldn't it be nice to go to Rome for dinner?"—until I finally took the job.

I stayed with TWA for four years in Kansas City and two more in New York before accepting a job as the chief financial officer at Bloomingdale's. I lasted a year. I found that I disliked retailing immensely. There were people there who were really concerned about where the men's socks were, and I just couldn't bring myself to care. When I received an offer to move back into the airline business, as chief financial officer at American Airlines, I jumped at it.

Later I became the chief marketing officer and was then named president of American in 1982, a time when the U.S. airline industry was facing a major crisis.

While commercial aviation has never been a successful industry and has recorded a cumulative loss of several billion dollars

ROBERT CRANDALL is the former chairman and chief executive officer of AMR Corporation and American Airlines. During his 25-year tenure at American, Crandall was instrumental in introducing several changes that revolutionized the travel industry. A native of Westerly, Rhode Island, Crandall is a graduate of the University of Rhode Island and the University of Pennsylvania's Wharton School. Crandall and his wife, Jan, live in Dallas. They have three adult children.

since it began, the crisis we faced at that time was unusually severe. It was a consequence of the Airline Deregulation Act of 1978.

From 1938 until 1978, commercial aviation in the U.S. was governed by an ever-growing morass of rules administered by the Civil Aeronautics Board. The CAB had been created to govern the developing air transportation industry and had long opposed both route expansion and price competition. The Deregulation Act did away with both the CAB and most of its rules—allowing airlines to choose whatever routes and fares they thought best.

This new freedom generated ferocious competition as new carriers entered the industry and established carriers expanded and modified their offerings. Most of the latter suffered large losses. American was in particularly dire straits.

The company had been losing market share for years and had a fleet and route system badly suited to a deregulated environment. Analysts marked American as a probable loser in the deregulation derby. It was clear we had to find a new solution—and quickly.

> Success is the product of integrity, preparation, dedication and focus.

The new airlines were able to keep both costs and fares low because they hired new employees at far lower pay rates and established much more flexible work rules than those in force at American and other established carriers. One obvious solution was to start and operate a separate, low-cost carrier. However, the unions that represented pilots, flight attendants and mechanics at all the established airlines would not allow any of the existing carriers to start a new airline not subject to existing contracts.

To overcome this problem, American came up with a compromise, which we dubbed "The Growth Plan." The idea was that we would grow American dramatically, thereby creating the equivalent of a new entrant carrier within American itself. To do so, we proposed that the unions permit us to hire new employees, in every category, at wage rates and work rules similar to those used by the new, startup airlines.

The payoff was that everyone would win. American's existing employees would benefit from increased job security and faster promotions. Growth would create new jobs for thousands of folks who would otherwise not have an opportunity to work for American, and shareholders would benefit from improved profitability.

It wasn't easy, but we eventually persuaded all of the unions to agree. And the plan worked. Between 1982 and 1985, we increased American's fleet from about 200 planes to more than 700. The company's route system expanded across the United States and into Canada, Mexico, Latin America, Europe and Asia. During the 1980s and 1990s, American was the most profitable of the major airlines. By the mid-1990s, American had become the world's largest airline and remains so today.

Creating and implementing "The Growth Plan" was the greatest accomplishment of my career. I have always felt—subject to the usual caveats about the need for reasonable intelligence and a little luck—that success is largely the product of integrity, preparation, dedication and focus.

To be successful in the airline industry requires lots of perspiration and a little inspiration as well. It's fast-paced, intellectually stimulating and deeply engrossing work. You need to be able to accurately identify problems, think carefully about the best possible solution, decide on a plan, marshal the best people you can find, provide sound leadership, and work like the devil to make it all happen.

I will never forget the night I was at a black-tie dinner party in Dallas when someone phoned to say that more than 50 of the aircraft on the ground at DFW had holes in them—a major hail storm had taken them out of service.

I rushed to the airport in my tux and spent the night helping our people reschedule the system, routing planes and crews—as best we could—to get the majority of our passengers where they needed to be. You don't get those kinds of challenges in most other businesses, which may explain why many who leave the industry eventually return, claiming boredom with whatever businesses lured them away.

WILLIAM E. DAVIS

One fall afternoon when I was in high school, I was shooting baskets in our backyard when Henry Whitbeck, an attorney and former state legislator who lived nearby, walked across the yard and asked if I had given any thought to attending one of the military service academies.

Even though many boys growing up in upstate New York dream of going to West Point, my honest answer was no. He explained that the local congressman, J. Ernest Wharton, wanted to nominate a candidate before he retired and that I should consider applying.

The more I thought about it, the more intrigued I became with the idea. The first determinant of success was your grade on an exam given by the congressman. I was pleased when my score placed me second in the district, but disappointed when I learned the first-place score was for a prep school student who had his heart set on going to West Point.

I was told that I could be the first alternate appointment to West Point, but that if the other student was admitted, I would be out of luck. My other choice was to accept an appointment to one of the other academies, and I picked the Naval Academy, even though I knew very little about the school or the navy.

WILLIAM DAVIS is the former chairman and chief executive officer of Niagara Mohawk Power Corporation, an electricity and natural gas utility in upstate New York. Prior to joining Niagara Mohawk, Davis was the executive deputy commissioner of the New York State Energy Office. A graduate of the Naval Academy, Davis worked aboard nuclear-powered Polaris submarines and as an instructor at the Academy. He also has a master's degree from George Washington University.

It turned out to be one of the best decisions of my life and a major turning point. The education I received there and the total experience I received in school and working in the nuclear submarine service was invaluable. Others have told me they marvel at my ability to stay focused and unflappable regardless of how drastic the situation seems, and my answer has always been, "Compared to plebe year, this is a piece of cake."

I spent nine years on active duty, which included 10 Polaris submarine patrols and a two-year stint teaching at the Academy, before my wife, Donna, and I concluded that my future career in the navy would likely include more sea duty than either of us would like. It was time to move into the private sector, so I went to work for the General Public Utilities Service Corp. in New Jersey.

While I was working as a project engineer for the construction of a nuclear power plant, I was offered a job by the state of New York, which allowed us to go back home, five miles from where Donna and I grew up. I was working for the state Commerce Department when the state created an Energy Office in 1976.

The office was brand new and had an important mission and a young, bright and exceptionally hard-working staff. Over a 13-year career in the office I was promoted to the executive deputy commissioner and had the chances to work with the governor's office, to testify before legislative hearings and to help produce the first State Energy Master Plan.

Over the years I received many calls about other job opportunities, and in 1989 such a call came from a search firm representing Niagara Mohawk, the largest and best known electric and gas utility in upstate New York. At that time, the company was suffering negative fallout from an expensive nuclear construction program. Schedule delays and cost overruns were threatening the company's reputation and its finances, as well as its relationship with the Public Service Commission and the governor's office.

I listened to their offer, but declined. They were persistent, however, and kept enhancing the offer until finally I reconsidered, agreeing to become vice president of corporate planning.

One evening in the fall of 1992, I was in my office in Syracuse when the company's chairman and CEO, Bill Donlon, walked in and shut the door behind him. I could tell something was going on, but I had no idea what he was about to say. He sat down and told me he had decided to retire.

What he said next really shocked me—he told me I should apply for his job. I didn't think there was any realistic way I would get the job—I was too far down the company's organizational ladder and had been with the company less than three years.

I had confidence in my ability to lead the company, however, so I took Bill's advice and applied. Still, it was a bit of a shock when he told me after the long evaluation process that I been selected for the job.

For the next 10 years, I served as chairman and CEO of Niagara Mohawk, the most challenging, exciting and rewarding period of my life. We overcame financial challenges, restructured the company and completed a merger with National Grid that made us part of one of the largest energy infrastructure companies in the world.

We had to make many tough decisions and cost-cutting moves, including trimming the work force from about 12,000 employees down to about 6,000. Those and other moves, however, were a matter of the company's survival.

What I learned in that job, as well as throughout my entire career, is that there are some very simple keys to success that really should go without saying but often don't.

The most important is to be honest. People want to surround themselves with people they know can be trusted. Working to develop a reputation for honesty is a job that never ends. If you become known as someone whose word can't be trusted, it's the kiss of death.

You also can't underestimate the importance of working hard. I honestly believe there is no more satisfying feeling in the world than a job well done.

Finally, treat those around you and the environment we live in with respect. You will be happier, and so will everybody else.

LYNN C. FRITZ

My family had owned a small freight forwarding company in San Francisco for more than 30 years when I began working there in 1965. I attended law school at night so I could work there during the day.

At that time the shipping business was very fragmented. Our company, named A.J. Fritz & Co. at the time, provided the documentation services required to import and export products through customs, primarily by ship. Various other companies performed a myriad of tasks required in that process—we only concentrated on that one particular, very small step. Comparatively speaking, we were a pimple on the neck of an elephant.

In the 1960s, there were literally thousands of small service companies located in every port and airport around the world that provided some narrow range of services to support international shipments.

The more I became familiar with the business, the more I realized that we and the other companies were not adding any value to process. A lot of steps had to be completed before a product even got to us, and a lot more steps had to be completed afterward to get the product where it needed to go. There was a lot of room for improvement. It just made sense to me that we should

Lynn Fritz was the chairman and CEO of Fritz Companies until May 2001, when it was acquired by UPS. Under his leadership, Fritz Companies was transformed from a small domestic documentation company to a global organization of 10,000 employees in 120 countries. A native of San Francisco, Fritz is a graduate of Georgetown University and earned a JD from Lincoln University School of Law.

try to take on the responsibility for more than just one of those steps.

The more parts of the process that we could control, I reasoned, the more sources of revenue that would bring to our company—and that would give us a distinct market advantage. A company, rather than having to contract with 20 or 30 companies to complete the entire shipping process, would be able to work with a smaller number of companies that provided the same services.

We started by trying to persuade our existing customers to let us handle more of their business. After all, they held the key to our success.

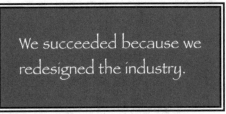

We succeeded because we redesigned the industry.

Combining services might have seemed like a great insight to us, but if the customers didn't want it, we were not going to be able to follow through on the idea.

It did require a leap of faith on the part of our customers. When you are working with multiple companies, you can always play one against the other—so this move would reduce their ability to change providers. Also, when you give all of your business to one company, it makes you much more vulnerable if something happens to that company.

Given that we had to prove the long-term value of our strategy, we knew we had to grow the business incrementally, and that was what we did. As we added more pieces of the business, we opened more offices in more cities to provide those services. In effect, we became first national customs broker. We were also the first company to introduce technology into the business. Previously, everything had been done manually. We automated the clearance process even before U.S. Customs—they adopted much of their programming from us.

When we added new clients, we opened offices in other cities specifically for them. We opened an office in the Twin Cities, for example, when we added 3M, and we did the same in Chicago when we added Mitsui.

The more we learned and understood about the entire shipping process, the more services we began to provide for our clients. One of our advantages was that we never owned our own planes or ships, and that allowed us to use multiple carriers and not to have to take on that added expense.

We began to go to our clients and basically say, "Let us become your shipping department. We know more about the business than you do, and we can provide that service better than you can do it yourself." Our position was that the more customers we had under our control, the more effectively we could negotiate with the carriers, and the better price we could get for both us and our clients. Thankfully, a lot of companies agreed and signed with us.

Our business continued to grow between seven percent and 15 percent every year for 20 years. We opened more markets and provided addi-tional services for an increas-ing number of customers and picked up fur-ther business from our existing customers.

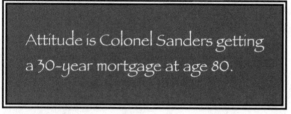

Attitude is Colonel Sanders getting a 30-year mortgage at age 80.

As we became more successful, the other companies throughout the industry had to follow our lead if they wanted to stay competitive. They had to change the way they operated. Our objective was "to redesign the industry" and, indeed, it resulted in a paradigm shift. Virtually all logistics providers and carriers throughout the world have now adopted this model.

The term I coined to describe the type of business we were operating was "integrated logistics." There really was not a word or phrase to describe this new full-service model, so we had to create one. Today, even local trucking companies are using this term to describe their services.

Our biggest breakthrough came in 1976, when we were able to add Sears, Wal-Mart and the military business from the Republic of China as clients. Signing those three clients really signaled to us that our idea was working.

Clearly, one of the keys to our success was the motivation of our employees. I always asked prospective employees what kind of position they would like to have. They were usually clear on the answer but had not been given the opportunity to perform. We called them "but if" people. What I tried to do was take away the "but if." I always believed in giving people a chance to see what they could do—and their response, dedication, and performance made our services special and distinguishable.

When we decided to sell the company to UPS in 2001, we had grown into a global organization with over 10,000 employees working in 120 countries around the world. UPS convinced me that selling the company would be in the best interest of our customers and employees. It was a highly complementary addition to their services and they agreed to take our entire population.

I would not have sold under any other conditions.

PETER GEORGESCU

I spent 37 years at Young and Rubicam, one of the largest advertising and marketing communications agencies in the world, retiring as CEO. During my tenure my team and I took the company public during a period that saw our revenues increase by 300 percent and profits by 900 percent. One doesn't have a career like this without a lot of help and a lot of breaks along the way.

My biggest break? That happened 50 years ago in Europe, long before I knew there was such a thing as advertising or marketing.

I was born and raised in Romania. Before the Second World War, my father had been a general manager for Standard Oil (now Exxon) in Romania's Ploesti oil fields, the richest oil reservoir in Europe. When the Nazis invaded, they arrested and imprisoned him as an enemy. Yet my parents were brave people. During his stay in prison, my dad, with the help of many patriotic Romanians and the allied forces through the OSS, planned and executed a coup against the Germans. As a result, when the Russians entered the country in early 1945, the Germans hardly put up a fight—but our Communist "liberators" turned out to be as bad as the Nazis.

When I was eight years old, two years after the end of the war, my father was free again and went back to work for the oil com-

PETER GEORGESCU is chairman emeritus of Young & Rubicam Inc., a network of preeminent commercial communications companies dedicated to helping clients build their businesses through the power of brands. He was the chairman and CEO of the company from 1994 through 2000. Georgescu spent 37 years at Young & Rubicam, joining the company after his graduation from Princeton and the Stanford Business School, where he earned his MBA. Georgescu emigrated from his native Romania in 1954 to live in the United States. He was inducted into the Advertising Hall of Fame in 2001.

pany. In the early winter of 1947, my parents took a scheduled trip
to Exxon's headquarters in New York. When it was time to return,
they weren't allowed back into Romania. The iron curtain had
descended around the new Soviet territory, which included our
homeland. The Communist putsch took hold, and now my parents were labeled dirty,
bourgeois imperialists
and evil capitalists—ene-
mies of the state.

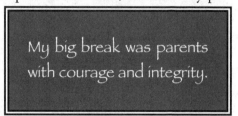

My big break was parents
with courage and integrity.

Dazed by all the tur-
moil, my brother Costa
and I were sent to live with my grandparents in Lipova, a small
town in Transylvania. We thought we would be safe there. The
house was a national treasure. It held my grandfather's 70,000-
book library and my grandmother's rooms full of Romanian peas-
ant costumes, beautifully embroidered. My grandfather—my
mother's father—had been a successful politician, the governor of
the Banat, the largest region of Romania's west. Yet in the new
Romania, he was also considered a potential insurgent like my
father.

Early one morning we found our two shepherd dogs dead in
the garden. They had been poisoned. We had no idea who had
done it or why. We went to bed that night mourning for them,
and just before daybreak awoke to the sound of boots on our mar-
ble floors—how I came to despise boots. The Communists had
burst into our home to arrest my 79-year-old grandfather. They
did the same with hundreds of thousands of Romania's intelli-
gentsia, generations of politicians and other would-be leaders. I
will never forget the serene face of my grandpa, trying to console
us, yet knowing he would never see us again. That terrible morning, I saw what evil can do, rising up in the most ordinary, otherwise benevolent hearts.

My brother and I, along with our grandmother, were taken
from Lipova and transported across the country to a town close to
the Russian border. We were given a series of humiliating, dangerous jobs, leaving for work at 6:00 a.m. and returning home 12
hours later, six days a week. I had to do the vilest tasks. I went into

the sewers to clear out sand and excrement. I was promoted to work for the local electric company, but I inherited the nightmare job no one else wanted, getting up at 4:00 a.m. to walk around in the dark, shutting down transformers. The transformers were housed in tall, metal cabinets. When my hand bumped into the wrong piece of bare metal, a searing jolt knocked me out cold.

I defended myself against dread and despair by becoming a stubborn, defiant worker, adapting to a work-camp meritocracy that existed only in my imagination. I forced myself to believe that if I worked hard enough, and well enough, I would be recognized and promoted, slowly earning the respect of my captors, maybe even my freedom.

It was a fantasy.

I was in denial, but as a result, I became a hard worker.

One day in March 1954, six years after we were taken captive, my brother and grandmother and I were told to pack up what little we had. It was time to leave. We had no idea whether we were heading toward freedom or deeper into captivity. The guards escorted us to meet the overnight train to Bucharest. Then, to our surprise, we were put on the next train to Austria and freedom.

The following morning, we arrived in Vienna. Our father met us on the platform. There was an instant of shock, we'd grown so much, but it was swept aside in a wave of excitement, tenderness and pleasure as we rushed into one another's arms. The next day, we flew to America, to New York. We were then reunited with our mother in another tearful, joyous embrace.

Like countless refugees before me, I began life anew in America. Our rescue made everything possible. But the part that means the most to me now is the way the rescue happened. Our father told us how, for six years, they had spent hundreds of thousands of dollars trying to save us, to no avail. One day a Romanian agent approached my parents and asked my father to spy for the Communists in exchange for the safety of our lives.

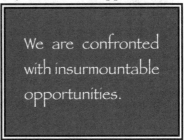

We are confronted with insurmountable opportunities.

My father, an influential executive and by this time a U.S. citizen, would have been in a position to do that, but after an agonizing night, with great trepidation, he and my mother decided to call the FBI. The agents who came to their house told them they had two choices. The first was to play along with the offer, and pretend to spy for the Communists, while American intelligence would actually be using them as double agents, feeding false information to the Romanians. Neither of them felt very comfortable becoming involved in the dubious ethics of a game like that. The second choice, and the one they chose, was to take their story to the press.

The idea behind taking the story to the press was that if they could create a large enough international scandal, it would force the Romanians and Russians to protect us. It was a dangerous plan. It could just as easily have provoked our captors into taking drastic action. It was the right thing to do, the ethical thing, but far riskier than collaboration with the enemy.

With the help of public relations experts from the FBI, the story of how we were being held hostage reached millions around the world. Newspapers, magazines and television covered the story. It provoked an outpouring of sympathy around the world.

Outraged by our plight and the Communists' craven attempt to use two innocent children as leverage for espionage, a ranking Republican on the House Foreign Relations Committee, Frances Payne Bolton, ambushed the Soviet foreign minister in an elevator after a United Nations meeting in 1953 and demanded our release. She and my parents continued to work behind the scenes, pushing for help.

In the end, President Eisenhower was believed to have traded some Soviet spies in exchange for the Georgescu boys. None of this was ever confirmed, but it was the story told around our home.

The breaks to follow weren't nearly as magical as my liberation from Romania, but there were many, all of them, in one way or another, smaller aftershocks of the first. I was generously allowed to join Exeter Academy, then earned my way into Princeton, and finally Stanford Business School. I was offered a job at Young and Rubicam right out of Stanford and stayed there for my entire career.

My big break was having parents with the courage and integrity to do the right thing. They spent one harrowing night debating whether they should spy on the American government to save the lives of their children, and chose instead to go to the authorities and then to the media with the truth. It might have resulted in a swift death for Costa and me, and maybe my grandmother. To them, however, it was the only genuine alternative to a life of shame.

Their leap of faith wasn't just the right thing to do: it worked. Their integrity, their courage, and honesty—in short, their example—became core values I tried to live by and to instill at Young and Rubicam. They were the values, ultimately, that enabled me to succeed.

JAMES J. HARFORD

M y wife, Millie, and I were having lunch in the Tuilerus Gardens in Paris in 1953 when I opened and read a letter from my brother Tom in New York. Tom knew my current job was about to come to an end and that we would soon be returning to the United States.

"Listen to this, Mil," I said, "Tom wants me to be interviewed for a job with the American Rocket Society."

Who had ever heard of the American Rocket Society? I knew I hadn't, which was probably one of the biggest reasons the letter went unanswered for a couple of weeks, until I received a second letter from my brother.

This time, Tom went into a little more detail about the job, even including a tear sheet of an article from *Colliers* magazine written by Wernher von Braun. In the article he talked about the possibilities for rockets and orbiting satellites, the exploration of the moon and other planets, and even establishing orbiting manned space stations. It also turned out that von Braun was on the board of directors of an organization known as the American Rocket Society.

My brother had become familiar with the group because he was selling advertising space for various aero publications and had just taken on the skinny *Journal of the American Rocket Society*.

JAMES HARFORD is the executive director emeritus of the American Institute of Aeronautics & Astronautics in Washington, D.C. A graduate of Yale with a degree in engineering, Harford was the executive secretary of the American Rocket Society from 1953 to 1963 and was a leading force in the merger of ARS with the Institute of Aeronautical Sciences. From 1964 through 1988 he was the executive director of AIAA.

"They need an executive director, Jim," he said. "They want an engineer who can write. That's you."

I was both an engineer and a writer, having spent the previous 16 months in Paris, traveling around France and writing articles under a pseudonym for a Paris magazine about how the United States was helping French industry recover under the Marshall Plan.

I was flattered by my brother's high opinion of me, and I was more than a little intrigued about the job after reading the magazine article. I had assumed I would apply for a job with a Fortune 500 company when I returned to the United States. Instead, here I was applying to work for an organization that had only two employees.

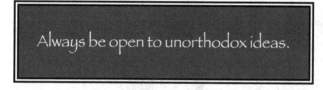

Always be open to unorthodox ideas.

I asked for a salary that was about four times what I had been making in Paris, $10,000 a year, and after an extensive interview by Dr. G. Edward Pendray, who was on the board of directors and was a former vice president of Westinghouse, I was offered and accepted the job.

One of the first tasks was to write a report that would be submitted to President Eisenhower recommending a satellite initiative by the United States. The report was well documented by scientific experts about all of the functions a satellite could perform—astronomical observation, earth resources studies, research on weightlessness and radiation in space, and global communications. This was information that 50 years later we all understand and have come to accept as routine. Back then, however, it read almost like a science fiction novel.

The President approved the plan, and the United States began developing a satellite program—only to be shocked when the Russians beat us into space by launching Sputnik in 1957. Nobody had any idea the Russian technology was that far advanced, and we had fully expected to be the first country to launch a satellite.

Instead, it turned out Russia not only had the first satellite but the first ICBM, launched the first dog into space, had the first man to go into space, the first woman, the first three-man crew, the first space walk, the first spacecraft to hit the Moon and then photograph its dark side, the first spacecraft to hit Venus and the first to fly by Mars.

Those successes by the Russian space program, however, only prompted United States officials to work even harder at building our program. We built a program that developed not only peaceful and military satellites but also spacecraft missions to every planet except Pluto, six missions sending 12 men to the Moon and back home again, and now we do have an operating space station in orbit.

The American Rocket Society grew with the interest in the space program and has since changed its name to the American Institute of Aeronautics and Astronautics. The organization now has 35,000 members and sections and student branches throughout the United States.

I don't think even my brother Tom had any idea that amount of growth would be possible when he wrote to me in Paris to encourage me to apply for the job, but I am glad he was persistent and insisted I ask for an interview.

The lesson that taught me, which I think is meaningful for anyone beginning or pursuing a career in any business, is that you should always keep an open mind to unorthodox ideas. Opportunities come up all the time that are unexpected and perhaps a bit unusual, but if you don't pursue and investigate them you will have no idea what you might be about to miss.

> Problems are created when reality is avoided—great leaders talk about tough topics.

RICHARD L. HUBER

One time in New York, not long ago, I was speaking with a group of talented and serious recent MBA graduates when one of them asked me, "Mr. Huber, perhaps you could tell us how you mapped out your career when you first started?"

I had to hold back my laughter.

After graduating from Harvard in 1959 with a degree in chemistry, I was so broke and in debt that I couldn't afford to travel very far to look for a job. To make matters worse, the oil and chemical industries were in a depressed state at that time and were not hiring new employees.

With both those factors in mind, I took the subway to downtown Boston to interview for the management training program at the First National Bank of Boston. During my college years, I had spent six months in Spain and had made some friends there who were from Argentina, which sounded to me like a mysterious and intriguing place. I really wanted to find a job that would allow me to move to Argentina, and First National Bank had had a large operation in that country for many years.

The training program lasted a little less than a year, during which time the Castro revolution in Cuba forced the company to close its sizable operations in that country. A number of seasoned,

RICHARD HUBER spent more than 40 years in the financial services industry and retired as the chairman, president and CEO of the Aetna insurance company in 2000. He began his career in 1959 with First National Bank of Boston and later worked in various international positions for Citibank. After working for Chase and Continental Bank, Huber joined Aetna in 1995 as vice chairman and chief financial officer. He now serves as the chairman and CEO of American Commercial Barge Line, the largest river transportation company in the United States. A graduate of Harvard, Huber and his wife are the parents of three sons and live in New York.

Spanish-speaking staff moved into other departments, including the company's offices in Argentina.

One morning as I was nearing the completion of the training program, the executive vice president in charge of international banking called me into his office. He told me that because of the reassignment of the officers expelled from Cuba to Argentina, it was unlikely that the bank would need any junior staff there for several years. But in view of my good performance in the training program, the bank would like to transfer me to its prestigious domestic banking operations.

For most employees, this was very much a desired place to work, but I was disappointed since my heart had been set on moving to Argentina. I thanked the executive for the offer, but told him that was not the reason I had joined the company, so I thought I would resign. He was quite surprised, but accepted my resignation and told me the steps I needed to follow, contacting the personnel office and so forth.

That afternoon, before I had a chance to get very far along in the process—or to think about what I would do for a job or what I was going to tell my new wife—the phone rang in my office. The executive vice president wanted to see me again. This time, he told me an audit team was going to Argentina for two months and they would like me to be a part of the team, even though I had no real accounting experience.

He added that there was no guarantee I would have a job offer at the end of the audit. Considering that I could see very little downside to the offer, however, I accepted it on the spot.

During those two months in Buenos Aires, I had numerous contacts with the bank's senior management, and at the end of the audit I was offered a job working on several new projects there. I spent the next five years in Buenos Aires working in a variety of jobs for the bank.

After returning to the main office in Boston for a year, I moved back to South America to become the deputy country head for Brazil. Two years later, at the age of 33, I was made the head of the bank's operations in Brazil and stayed there for close to a decade, eventually joining Citibank and heading its banking operations in the country before moving on to positions in Japan and finally New York.

I have often wondered what would have happened had I not received the offer to join the audit team going to Argentina, but I know I definitely would have been out on the street, looking for a job. My career could have gone a totally different direction, or I could have ended up on welfare. I was glad I never had to worry about that.

It was interesting that I ended up working in the banking business since I had never gone to business school. Perhaps due to that fact, most of my insight and understanding of business came from my own experiences, not from what I had been taught in school.

During my years in Japan and New York, I was actively involved in Citibank's training and recruitment programs. When I took over the Japan operations, Citibank was the largest foreign bank in Japan, but it was in a petrified state, not having recruited any new employees for nine years. I realized immediately how deadly that could be—it was killing the organization by not bringing in new blood.

When I took over the Asian operations, in effect we began over-hiring people, but it was key to the growth of the company.

Another important factor to the success of both the company and the individual is reputation. Adhering to the highest ethical standards possible is of prime importance. I even followed this principle in countries as notorious for corruption as Indonesia, China, the Philippines and Brazil. Eventually, the reputation for not playing the corruption game became one of my most valuable personal assets.

My response to that group of MBA graduates in New York was that, for most people, a career path is more like a random walk than a carefully mapped path. I definitely fell into the former category. My advice is to put yourself out in traffic as much as possible and be willing to take risks even if it means reaching well above what you think is your current level of competency.

Don't be afraid to fail.

LARRY JOHNSTON

Ibegan my career with GE in 1972, directly after graduating from college—and it was then that my education truly began. The opportunities and rewards came very fast, and included stops in places like Charlotte, Raleigh, Louisville, Washington D.C., and Cleveland. In one 12-year stretch I built six houses.

It was all so challenging and exciting I never gave it a second thought. At age 39, I was elected a corporate officer and named the vice president of Sales & Distribution for GE Appliances, a global business. I loved the job and was content to stay there for the rest of my career.

Those plans changed two years later, however, when I got a phone call from Bill Conaty, the chief of human resources, with an urgent message from Jack Welch, the CEO, and Jeff Immelt, the CEO of GE's Medical business.

"Larry, call Jack and Jeff as soon as you can," Bill said. "They want you to consider moving to Paris to run GE-Medical Europe. They need someone there as soon as possible."

GE-Medical Europe was notorious for being one of GE's biggest leadership challenges. Years earlier, following the acquisition of RCA, Jack and Paolo Fresco had pulled off a coup by trading the RCA Television business to a state-owned French company for a large sum of cash plus their European Medical Imaging

LARRY JOHNSTON is the chairman of the board, CEO and president of Albertsons, Inc., one of the world's largest food and drug retailers. The company has more than 230,000 employees in 2,500 stores across the United States. Prior to joining Albertsons in 2001, Johnston spent 28 years at General Electric in a variety of leadership positions. He served as president and CEO of GE Appliances, a multibillion-dollar global business, from 1999 to 2001. Johnston is a graduate of Stetson University and lives in Boise, Idaho.

business, which was then number four in Europe. The European medical business was the platform GE needed to finally challenge Siemens and Phillips for leadership in Europe and to eventually make GE the undisputed leader in diagnostic imaging in the United States, Asia and Europe.

It was a great concept, but it wasn't working. Ten years and three CEOs later, the business was still number four in Europe and was losing more than $100 million a year.

Looking back, it was a scary move, but it turned out to be a big break for me. Jeff Immelt had become the new head of GE's Worldwide Medical business. At Appliances, one of GE's toughest global businesses, we had worked side by side—he had been VP of market-

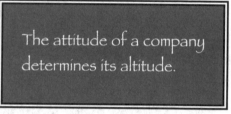

The attitude of a company determines its altitude.

ing when I was VP of sales—so I jumped at the chance to work with Jeff again.

The only part of the job that worried me was being able to master the language, so I enrolled in a French immersion class in Paris that met from 8:00 a.m. until 5:00 p.m. five days a week for a month. To keep a focus on my business, I then worked with my management team from 5:00 p.m. until midnight.

I definitely believe that the attitude of a company or organization determines its altitude. I am a strong believer in positive thinking. Those are the kinds of people I want working on my team.

I brought in a new leadership team of 20 key players from 13 countries. We diversified the company by making more than 20 acquisitions and formed several joint ventures in less than three years. We moved into new business segments such as imaging services, medical software, cardiac ultrasound and hospital supplies. We sold the radiation therapy business and endured a 57-day strike. We fought the French government on the 35-hour work week and we closed factories in France and Belgium and moved the work to low-cost countries like Hungary, India and Mexico. We launched a Six Sigma Quality initiative and introduced new blockbuster digital imaging products in mammography and cardiac as well as new 3D software that allowed vascular surgeons to save patients from life-threatening aneurism.

After those first three years we had grown the business by 75 percent. We'd moved from number four in Europe to number two, and had turned the $100 million loss into a $100 million profit.

Along the way, I also proved to myself that leadership skills are portable regardless of the industry, that you don't have to be a technology expert to run a high-tech business, and that living and working in a foreign country is very doable.

During the third year of my European assignment Jack added the responsibility of chairman GE-Europe to my duties, asking me to coordinate best practices among all GE's European businesses. At the end of that year, he then asked me to return to the United States to become president and CEO of GE Appliances. Twenty-eight years earlier I had started as a trainee in that division, so I felt this was a return home.

In 2001, my old friend Jeff Immelt replaced Jack as chairman and CEO. I also began to receive calls from other companies and eventually left GE to become chairman and CEO of Albertsons, Inc., the 35th largest company in the United States—a $36 billion food and drug retailer with 2,500 stores and 230,000 employees.

It is a little different living in Boise, Idaho, instead of Paris, but it is a beautiful city and the leadership challenge is no less significant. Many of the lessons I learned with GE have proved invaluable to me on a daily basis since joining Albertsons, a company that began with the opening of a single store 65 years ago in Boise by Joe Albertson.

Looking back, it would have been an easy decision to turn down the job offer in Paris, because the challenge seemed insurmountable. A chance to succeed where others had failed in one of the greatest companies in the world, however, was too much to ignore. The moral of the story is clear: Tough challenges, characterized by seemingly impossible tasks, are the opportunities that allow you to stretch and learn like no other.

DONALD R. KEOUGH

I was lucky enough to receive some great advice from my parents while I was in high school. I was attending an all-boys Catholic high school, and everyone was given the opportunity to sign up for one extracurricular activity. Out of all the choices I picked "tumbling," even though all I knew about it was that you jumped up and down a lot.

When my mother checked my records, she asked, "What is tumbling?"

I told her it was a gym activity in which you jumped up and down.

"Are you going to do a lot of tumbling in your life?" she asked me.

When I said no, she looked down at the list of choices and pointed her finger at "debating."

I never tumbled the rest of my life, but I did do a lot of debating.

During that time, I also began working for my father, who had a cattle commission firm in the Sioux City, Iowa, stockyards. One of my jobs was to roam the stockyards and buy "retired" bulls for a meat packing company back East. The first two days I listened to the salesmen tell me what a wonderful animal it was— and I watched the man instead of the bull.

DON KEOUGH is chairman of the board of Allen & Company Inc., a New York investment banking firm. He was elected to that position in 1993 after retiring as president, chief operating officer and a director of The Coca-Cola Company. His tenure with the company dated back to 1950 and he was president from 1981 until his retirement. A graduate of Creighton University, Keough and his wife live in New York.

My father took me aside and told me, "When you are buying anything, examine the merchandise and pay very little attention to the presentation of it."

Throughout my career, that simple thought was always in the back of my mind. I probably participated in the buying of hundreds of millions of dollars of advertising—paying no attention to the pitch. Even though the pitch was coming from very articulate and creative people, my eyes were glued on the advertising, thanks to my dad's lesson.

My parents' advice served me well throughout my entire career.

When I was a young man working in advertising and marketing for a coffee company in Omaha, Nebraska, it seemed as if I was always leaving home early in the morning for work and coming home late at night. My wife, Mickie, and I had four kids, and they would often regale me about the fun they had had that day with our neighbor who lived across the street.

> The rate at which organizations learn becomes a sustainable competitive advantage.

He and his wife had three children of their own. I did not know what his job was, but I knew he didn't leave the house often and he had plenty of time to play with his—and my—kids. My children loved him. They played with his train set, went to the park, and simply had fun.

It was around 1960 when he came over one day for a visit. He said he was starting an investment fund with three or four of his friends and wanted to know if I would be interested. He said maybe he could help get my kids through college.

"Look, I'm working on grade school right now. I will get around to college later," I replied.

He said that his friends were putting $10,000 apiece into the fund, and that he would love to have me join them.

While I did not have the $10,000 at the time, I knew I could have borrowed it from my father. As I told Mickie, however, I just didn't feel comfortable entrusting $10,000 to a man who didn't get up and go to work every day.

Well, that man's name was Warren

> Make a decision—stick with it—and more forward.

Buffett, and had I made a different decision that day, I know the rest of my life would have changed significantly. Still, I've never looked back, and my family has remained lifelong friends of Warren, his wife, Susie, and their family. We are very close, and I am privileged to be on the board of Berkshire Hathaway, the company Warren founded and leads.

In addition to the advice given to me by my parents, I can also pass along this lesson: Once you make a decision, you should move forward and never look back.

In 1959, the company I was working for, Paxton & Gallagher Co., was sold to the Swanson family of TV dinner fame. We were then bought by the Texas-based Duncan family, who ran a large and successful coffee business. Then, in 1962, Duncan Foods was sold to the Coca-Cola Company.

I never changed businesses. I started in 1950, kept my head down and went to work. Every new owner gave me an opportunity to grow, and I felt privileged to work for each of them.

As I have often said, I jumped into a little creek, which became a river, which turned into a gulf, which grew into an ocean.

All I ever did was swim.

SIDNEY KIMMEL

My father was a musician, and in the years before the Depression, he had a fairly lucrative business. All that changed, of course, when the country's economy collapsed and nobody was spending a nickel on a band. We were broke.

He took a job as a cab driver, only to find out nobody was taking cabs. They were walking or staying home.

Because of those trying times, I became very aware of financial concerns at an early age. I also came to appreciate how generous my father was—even though he didn't have much, he always was sharing with somebody he thought was worse off than him. I never will forget the time somebody gave him a $50 tip—a huge amount, especially in those days—and even though we barely had enough money to get by, he gave half of the tip to another driver who was struggling.

I really had no idea what I was going to do with my life—there certainly wasn't a family business to step into—but I did make up my mind that, whatever I did, I was going to work hard enough to become financially secure. When I was old enough, I didn't want to go to college, I wanted to go right into work and start making money.

One of the jobs I applied for was with the Voice of America. I didn't hear from them for three months, and when they called,

SIDNEY KIMMEL is the chairman of the board and founder of Jones Apparel Group, Inc., a Fortune 500 company and one of the world's leading designers and marketers of branded apparel, footwear and accessories. The company's brands include Jones New York, Polo Jeans Co., Nine West, Evan-Picone, Gloria Vanderbilt, Anne Klein, Kasper, Easy Spirit and l.e.i. Kimmel founded the Sidney Kimmel Foundation and its subsidiary, the Sidney Kimmel Foundation for Cancer Research, in 1993. Since that time the Foundation has awarded more than $420 million to various philanthropic causes. His film company, Sidney Kimmel Entertainment, is now one of the leading independent producers in the film industry.

the message was that they didn't have a job for me. Based on the results of several aptitude tests I had taken, however, they thought I would be a good candidate for a job at the State Department.

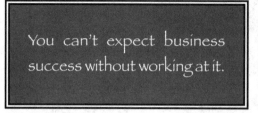

You can't expect business success without working at it.

They wanted me to train as a cryptographer in the Washington, D.C., code room, so off I went.

At the end of the yearlong program, I got word that I was about to be drafted. I told the Draft Board that I thought my work as a cryptographer should give me a draft exemption, but they said no. They did offer to allow me to go in as a captain in the signal corps, instead of as a private—but captains were going straight to the front and were getting killed every day.

I chose to decline their offer.

After the war, I wound up in New York and wanted to return to Philadelphia. I was working at a knitting mill, knitting men's sweaters. After two years, I moved on to a new company called The Villager, which was a women's clothes designer.

I really enjoyed the creative side of designing clothes. I liked the challenges of working with colors and silhouettes. I then got involved in the production of clothing and was pleased with how my career was going.

After 10 years working for The Villager, the company was sold and I suddenly found myself out of a job. The clothing business was all I knew, so I made the decision to start my own company.

I was preparing to do just that in January of 1970 when I was contacted by the W.R. Grace Co. They were a major company and had recently acquired a clothing business. Their executives knew nothing about the clothing industry, and they asked me to work as a consultant to see if I could fix the company and turn it around.

I agreed to do it on the one condition that I would also proceed with starting my own company, which we named Jones New York. I also got an agreement with W.R. Grace that, if they decided to divest itself of the clothing business, I would have the right of first refusal to purchase the company.

This arrangement really allowed me to grow my business. I owned 50 percent, and it was doing quite well. People liked our designs and styles, and that was the side of the business I enjoyed the most.

I once did an interview with a business magazine writer and casually admitted during our three-hour conversation that I could not even read a balance sheet. That of course turned out to be the headline of a two-page article, and made me even more determined to better understand all aspects of the business. The more I learned, the better the business performed.

The challenge over the years, as we acquired more labels and kept expanding, was to become stronger. The stronger your business, the easier it is to maintain your position. In 1985, I bought out my partner for $9 million for his half of the company so I could become the sole owner. When we took Jones New York public in 1991, we were doing about $800 million a year in sales. Today, our annual sales are about $4.5 billion, and we now have approximately 15,000 employees.

Because our business has done so well, it has made it easy for me to become more involved with many worthwhile, charitable

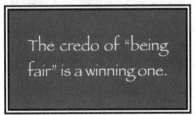

The credo of "being fair" is a winning one.

causes. I've always said that my ultimate goal is to help find a cure for cancer, and while we still have not accomplished that, I am proud of the funding we have been able to provided for research that is being directed toward that goal. We've established four cancer centers around the country: the Sidney Kimmel Comprehensive Cancer Center at Johns Hopkins; the Sidney Kimmel Urologic and Prostate Center at Memorial Sloan Kettering; the Sidney Kimmel Cancer Center in San Diego; and the Sidney Kimmel Cancer Center at Jefferson Hospital in Philadelphia.

I know one of the keys to my success has been hard work. I don't play golf and no longer play tennis, so my leisure time has been spent working. I am not saying people should never get away from their work, but you can't expect to succeed at a business if you are not working at it. Just as importantly, however, another key to my success has been luck. Anybody who doesn't think that luck plays a role in someone's success is lying to themselves.

My credo has always been to be fair. It is easy being a fair and a nice guy, and I know one thing, it sure feels right. A lot of people you'll meet in the business world, though, are not nice people. It may sound strange, but I have never felt like I had to take the last nickel off the table. I just wanted to get a fair deal.

KENNETH LANGONE

If there is a thin line between audacity and folly, I remember that late winter day in 1968 when it looked as if I had crossed it.

I was working for R.W. Pressprich & Co., an investment bank and brokerage in New York. I had started with them as a salesman in 1962, and four years later was made a partner just after turning 30 years old. The company was primarily a bond house for railroads and was considered the leading firm in the country in terms of dealing with railroad acquisitions and mergers.

Where I saw the potential growth for the company was in high-tech areas. We had done some work with taking companies public with a stock offering, but had not completed any major deals.

Rumor had it that Ross Perot, who already had developed a very big reputation in the business world, was thinking about taking his company public. Working through a mutual friend, Jack Hight, I was able to arrange a 30-minute meeting with Perot at his office in Dallas. I had 48 hours to prepare for that meeting, and in that short period I learned as much as I could about Perot and his company.

I had been forewarned that I was to be prompt, not to go over my allotted time, and not to use any profanity. I knew Perot had a reputation for being fair and honest. I also knew he didn't have

KENNETH LANGONE is the founder and chairman of Invemed Associates L.L.C., a New York Stock Exchange member firm engaged in investment banking and brokerage. A graduate of Bucknell University, Langone earned his MBA from New York University's Stern School of Business. He is a co-founder of Home Depot, Inc., and serves on the boards of various corporations and charities. Langone and his wife, Elaine, have three grown sons.

much time for small talk, or for boaster who promised more than they could deliver. So I was as prepared as I could be when I walked into his office.

Had I been there just for insight, I'd say our conversation went well. Everything I had been told about Perot was confirmed. He was canny about the business world and astute about politics. I wasn't there for insight, however. I was there to make a pitch to him about our company's banking services. He spent almost my entire time allotment talking about what he had heard from my competitors on Wall Street about the cloudy prospects for his company.

With about one minute to go before I knew I would be ushered out the door, he asked me for my opinion. I told him I didn't think I could answer that question in the time I had left, but he told me to proceed. Since I was already breaking one of the rules I had been given, I decided to go all the way and give him some direct New York candor. I told Perot that worries about how to go public were only imagined. I said the anxieties that so many private CEOs had about which investment bank was the most prestigious were, in Texas parlance, BS.

> I learned at an early age to "be myself."

Our meeting continued for the next 13 hours—and it was as lively and candid a conversation as I have ever had. The end result was that he decided to delay the public offering while he learned more about the business and about me. He said what was most important to him was that he was doing business with me as a person, and that I had to be on the top, on the bottom and in the middle of all the arrangements.

I think I was able to demystify the entire process for him so he felt more comfortable about the decisions he was making. I recall early on he said he would like to see the prospectuses of previous deals I had done. There were none.

Was I being audacious or foolhardy?

Here I was going after one of the most sought-after pieces of business in the country with no experience doing that type of business. Instead of telling me to get lost, though, Perot listened to me and to my ideas. I assured him that it was my company that was taking all of the risk. If we failed at this, we would be wiped out. He would still have a very viable company.

After three months, Perot agreed to give my bank the business and the public offering sprang forth as planned.

I believe Perot trusted me not only because of my frankness but also because I was personally committed to giving full effort to the details of our deal. I didn't delegate even the smallest matters to assistants, but handled everything—returning phone calls, writing handwritten letters, everything—myself.

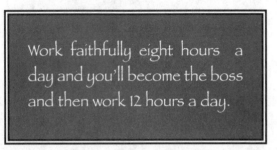

Work faithfully eight hours a day and you'll become the boss and then work 12 hours a day.

I told Perot that I believed we could raise 100 times the firm's earnings with the public offering. That was a high number, given that most of the other companies he was talking with were only pledging 70 times earnings. We did it too, actually reaching 116 times earnings. It was the defining moment of my career.

The lessons I learned from Perot have stayed with me ever since. I learned to be myself, as basic a lesson as there is—yet the one that we keep forgetting as we put on our masks and poses and tell ourselves that such foolery is working.

Everyone is a composite of pluses and minuses, virtues and flaws. Trouble starts when we try to hide the negatives, which becomes the worst negative of all.

The other lesson I learned was the importance of the follow-through. Over the years I have met too many people, from board rooms to living rooms, who don't follow through. They go back on their word. You can't believe half of what they say, and of the other half, you have grave doubts. Worse, they will let a strong idea languish.

Accomplishment is all about follow-through. No matter how small or insignificant you may think a task is, make sure it is done and done right. If you take care of the small things, the big things will take care of themselves. A lot of business people think some tasks are beneath them, like returning phone calls. They think they don't have to do that any more. It's a result of self-importance. The mundane tasks seem beneath you and what appears trivial gets quickly ignored.

In reality, though, reputation is built with those small, ordinary bricks. Life is all about people. I have never invested in a company where I didn't feel good about the people involved.

ARTHUR LEVITT

When I was growing up, my father always stressed to me the importance of "loving what you do." He was a lawyer, but he discouraged me from following in his footsteps because he didn't believe the amount of work was commensurate with the compensation.

Both of my parents had a profound impact on my life. They taught me always to strive for success and to stand up for the "little guy." They emphasized that a good name was the finest legacy I could leave my children.

I never really had a particular dream of what I wanted to do. I like challenges, and I like diversity, and I've enjoyed every job I've had except one. By temperament I am very curious, and the opportunity to shift gears and do something new and different always attracted me.

Over the years, I worked as a retail representative for *Life* magazine, took a job in the business department of *Time*, sold cattle and ranch land, helped found a securities firm (Cogan, Berlind, Weill and Levitt), served as the chairman of the New York Economic Development Corporation, was chairman of the American Stock Exchange, and started a publishing company that owned *Roll Call*, the newspaper that covers Capitol Hill. All of those jobs came before I accepted my greatest challenge, becoming

ARTHUR LEVITT served as the 25th chairman of the U.S. Securities and Exchange Commission. Appointed by President Clinton in 1993, he was reappointed to a second term in 1998 and served as the chairman until 2001, becoming the longest serving chairman in the history of the Commission. Levitt earlier served as chairman of the New York City Economic Development Corp., chairman of the American Stock Exchange and owned *Roll Call*, a newspaper covering Capitol Hill.

the chairman of the U.S. Securities and Exchange Commission in 1993.

Two individuals greatly influenced my professional life. The first was an English teacher in high school, Miles Kastendieck, who taught me to develop a critical sense, the ability to distinguish the ordinary from the superb. The other was my boss at *Time*, Nicholas Samstag, who taught me to seek excellence and to settle for nothing less. He taught me a great deal about sales promotion and how to motivate people. He taught me never to settle for anything other than the best. He taught me to take chances, to test the water, to think beyond the box, to consider the outrageous and make the impossible possible.

What had not seemed possible to me previously was that I could become a good salesman. My first job after coming out of the Air Force in 1954 was working as a retail representative for *Life* magazine in Cincinnati, Ohio. My responsibility was to call on department stores, supermarkets, drug stores, tire retailers, jewelry chains, and so on to attempt to persuade them to display "As advertised in *Life*" point of purchase signs next to the appropriate merchandise.

I worked alone, out of my home, and after about eight weeks of rejections I was ready to quit. An experienced space salesman who was my boss, David Borie, came to town from his office in Detroit and persuaded me to stay. "Call on five people—the five who gave you the hardest time, who wouldn't see you or hung up on you—every day for the next two months," he said. He told me if I could get through that period, faithfully making the calls, I would become a great salesman.

> Life is a grindstone—whether it grinds you down or polishes you up, depends on you.

It turned out he was right. The experience taught me not to be deterred by rejection, and my work impressed my bosses enough that they transferred me to the main office in New York, where I was assigned to work in public relations for *Time*.

It was the only job in my life I didn't really like because I found it boring, and after eight months I was able to transfer to the promotions department, where I got the chance to work for Nicholas.

A friend helped me get into the business of selling cattle and ranch land, and another friend led me to a new securities firm that was opening in 1961. That firm eventually grew to become the third largest brokerage firm in the country, and I left it to run the American Stock Exchange, where I stayed for 12 years.

> Every new job is a broadening experience.

All of the jobs were very different, but in a way I think they all helped prepare me to be the chairman of the SEC. President Clinton appointed me to the job in 1993, and I served in that capacity until 2001.

It was far and away the most rewarding and interesting job of my life. It was a job where you could make a difference and change behavior. You could take ideas and translate them into reality. My top priority was investor protection, and we worked to educate, empower and protect America's investors. Among other accomplishments, we were able to reform the debt markets, improve broker sales and pay practices, promote the use of plain English in investment literature and encourage foreign companies to list on U.S. markets.

I always thought opportunities came along every day. I accepted every job that was offered to me except one, and I never regretted any of those decisions. Luck probably accounted for more than half of whatever professional success I experienced, and prevented me from stumbling into errors I might easily have made.

PETER LYNCH

People have often said some of the best business tips they ever received came on the golf course. That certainly was true for me. In 1955, when I was 11 years old, I began working as a caddy at a very nice golf course in West Newton, Massachusetts, near Boston. I caddied for many corporate executives, and while they played, they discussed what stocks they were buying or selling. I remembered the names and kept looking in the newspaper weeks and months later to see how they were doing.

As the stocks went up, I remember thinking, "Gee, this makes a lot of sense." Of course, I didn't have any money to invest, but I became interested in watching the stock market at that young age.

My interest continued to grow as I finished high school and moved on to Boston College, and by this time I had been able to save a little money. My attention was drawn to the air freight industry after reading an article for one of my classes. Through research I found a company called Flying Tiger. When I was a sophomore, in 1963, I bought my first stock, investing $1,000 at $7 a share in Flying Tiger.

The company did very well, but not for the reasons I expected. I thought the air cargo industry was going to take off, and it did, but primarily because of the Vietnam War. Flying Tiger made a fortune shuttling troops and cargo into and out of the Pacific.

PETER LYNCH is considered one of the most successful money managers in Wall Street history. He ran Fidelity's Magellan Fund from 1977 until 1990, and during that period it was the number-one fund in the world. Lynch stopped running the Magellan Fund to devote more time to his wife, Carolyn, and their three daughters. Today he is vice chairman of Fidelity Management & Research Company and serves on several boards of charities, offering assistance to museums, hospitals, schools and libraries. A graduate of Boston College, Lynch earned his MBA from The Wharton School at the University of Pennsylvania. He is the author of three books, including *One Up on Wall Street* and *Beating the Street*.

In less than two years, the stock was selling for $32 a share. Over the next few years I sold off some of my shares and used those funds to pay for graduate school. I often joked that I went to grad school on a Flying Tiger scholarship.

When the price of the stock went up, it was a good feeling. I don't know what would have happened to my career if that stock had bombed, and I was glad I never had to find out.

When I was a senior, my caddying experience again paid off for me. For 10 years I had caddied for the president of Fidelity, Mr. Sullivan. They had three summer openings, and he said to me, "Why don't you apply?" They had 75 applicants for the three positions, but I was lucky enough to be hired for one of the jobs.

Fidelity was and still is a great company. They had done such a great job marketing mutual funds that even my widowed mother was investing $100 a month into Fidelity Capital. It didn't take me long to learn the secrets of the company's success. They had embraced the philosophy that you preserve capital by purchasing companies whose profits are going to improve or grow nicely over several years.

Summer interns were assigned to research companies and write reports. I was assigned to the paper and publishing industry and set out across the country visiting these companies. Since the airlines were on strike, however, the company I learned the most about was Greyhound.

After two years in the army, I rejoined Fidelity as a full-time employee in the research department in 1969. In 1974 I was promoted from assistant director to the director of research, and the Dow Jones lost 250 points in the next three months. In May 1977, I took over the Fidelity Magellan fund.

The fund had $20 million in assets, built on a portfolio of 40 stocks. Ned Johnson, one of my bosses, suggested that I reduce the number to 25 stocks. I listened politely, then went out and increased the portfolio to 60 stocks. Six months later, we were up to 100 stocks and soon thereafter, 150 stocks.

I didn't make that decision to be obstinate, but I honestly believed I was more comfortable working with a larger number of stocks. We did all of the research necessary on the different companies. When I saw a bargain, I couldn't resist buying it—and in those days there were bargains everywhere. My philosophy has always been that the more companies you look at, the more good ones you are going to find.

Tips and ideas can come from anywhere. I remember one time being at Sears and asking them what departments were doing well. He said carpets had been great for three weeks—so I spent the next two days researching carpet stocks. It's easy to figure out if carpets are selling well at Sears, they are probably selling well for other companies as well.

In this business, if you are right six or seven times out of 10, you are doing terrific. You need a couple of the stocks to do really well—you have to let the big ones make up for your mistakes, and you have to be willing to take some risks.

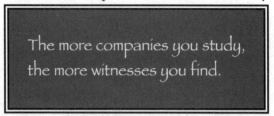

The more companies you study, the more witnesses you find.

Working with stocks is kind of like being a fan watching a football game. Whatever you do won't affect the outcome of the game. You can buy a stock in a car company, but that won't make the company sell more cars. As an investor, you are not going to invent the minivan, but you will be able to enjoy the benefits of that invention.

What I have learned in my career is that the secret to success is to surround yourself with bright folks and give them freedom and responsibility. You don't want to work for somebody who tells you how to do something and says you can't do this or that. You don't want to work for somebody who second-guesses you. They can second guess the results, but not the way you did your job.

After 13 years of running the Magellan Fund, I realized that was enough. I missed being home to watch our children grow up. I was 46 and ready to move on to the next phase of my life.

GAVIN MACLEOD

Ialways wanted to be an actor, even deciding to leave my high school football team when I had a chance to perform in my first major play, *The Royal Family*. After graduating with a degree in fine arts from Ithaca College, I was on my way to New York, where I had a chance to study acting with Frank Corsaro from The Actor's Studio.

One day after class, Frank told me he was doing a new play, *A Hatful of Rain*, and asked if I would be interested in understudying. I immediately said yes and asked when I could start. Frank said he would be in touch.

Time passed, and I heard nothing from him. Frank left town with the show, and eventually it opened in New York and became a smash hit. My wife, a Rockette at Radio City Music Hall, and I saw it in its first week and were very impressed with the production. Walter Winchell called it "the best acting on a New York stage."

Meanwhile, I had gone back to work at my day job, as a cashier at Jim Downey's Steak House, which was a major gathering place for the acting crowd, thinking that maybe Frank had forgotten about his job offer to me. My wife was pregnant at that time, so I was getting kind of desperate, even though I had done four off-Broadway shows and made one appearance on CBS-TV.

GAVIN MACLEOD has been a professional actor for more than half a century. He has appeared on stage, film and television productions throughout the world, gathering many awards. Since 1986, MacLeod has been the spokesperson for Princess Cruises. He and his wife, Patti, host a program, *Back on Course*, on Trinity Broadcasting Network. They have seven children and nine grandchildren.

Then, in 1955, I received the big news that Tony Franciosa was leaving *Hatful* to go make a film on the West Coast. I was told they were going to be holding auditions for understudies. I knew I had to get in touch with Frank and remind him of our earlier conversation.

I was at work behind the cash register at lunch one day when I looked up and saw Frank leaving the restaurant. I left my post and chased after him, calling out to him. He stopped and greeted me with an "Oh yes, yes," when I reminded him what he had said months earlier.

That opening got me an audition to read for the show, and I ended up getting the job, my first Broadway experience, where I had the chance to work with some of the most accomplished and exciting people in the business, including Shelly Winters, Ben Gazzara and Harry Guardino. I spent a year and a half in the show in New York and touring, and it was a wonderful experience.

I don't know what would have happened to my career if I had not made an effort to call out to Frank that day outside of the restaurant. I just happened to be in the right place at the right time and took the risk that he would remember me and our conversation.

That play opened a lot of doors for me. I was not going to tour when it left New York, but the actor who was going to take my spot was not working out and the producers asked me to reconsider. I talked it over with my wife and we finally decided I should do it.

I was able to move to the West Coast in 1957, just as television was beginning to gain in popularity, and that was another case of being in the right place at the right time. I met many wonderful people who would be instrumental in my career and development as an actor.

Acting, or the show business profession in general, is really no different than many other lines of work. You have to be lucky to get an opening, and then you have to be good enough at what you do to take advantage of that opening and show your bosses that you can do the job. The better you do at that job, the more responsibilities you will earn and you will keep progressing higher throughout your career.

One of the biggest factors in this business is that so much of what determines your success lies outside of your control. You can be a great actor, but if you are in a show that nobody watches and that the critics don't like, your chances of survival are not very good. I've seen some of the best shows on television canceled after only three weeks.

I tell young people, especially those interested in acting, that you had better become an inflatable balloon, because you are going to get knocked down all the time and you have to be able to bounce right back up. It's an exciting field, but it can humble you in a hurry.

That shouldn't keep you from taking risks in this business, however. I think Teddy Roosevelt once said that he "would rather have a man who tried and failed than have a man who never tried at all." I believe he was right.

When I was a kid, riding on a carousel, there were gold rings that

> Have goals—keep striving.

everyone tried to reach for. If you were lucky enough to grab one and hold onto it, you were entitled to a free ride. I have tried to teach that simple lesson to our seven children—if you don't risk reaching for that gold ring, you will never get it.

After I had already found a great deal of success, especially with *The Mary Tyler Moore Show*, I decided to take on the role of the captain on *The Love Boat*. Every critic said the show was going to sink like the Titanic, but I didn't believe them. I thought it was going to be a hit, and it turned out I was right. The show ran for 10 years and catapulted me into the role of an unofficial goodwill ambassador for the United States.

You have to have goals, and even though your goals sometimes change, you still have to keep striving for them. There are many more things I want to accomplish in my life. I am 73 years old, but I still have dreams.

JAMES L. MANN

From an early age I was fascinated by computers. In the early 1960s, there were not many people who could make that statement. There were far more people who were afraid of the approaching computer age than excited by it, but I was fascinated by the possibilities.

When I was first learning how to program a computer, I doubt if there were 10,000 people in the world who knew how to do what I was doing. It wasn't that I was smarter or more intelligent than anyone else, it was just an area of business that I found interesting and wanted to learn more about.

I kind of got into the business by accident. Trying to find a job after four and a half years in the air force, I applied at IBM. The company was developing the first generation of computers at the time, and they gave everybody who applied for any job a programming aptitude test. I scored very well and got the job.

This was a much better job than my first work experiences years earlier, when I earned money by picking up empty soda bottles from underneath the bleachers of a semipro softball stadium and setting pins at the employee bowling alley of a local electric company. The only lessons I took with me from those jobs was that no matter what job you have, you should always do the best you can.

JIM MANN served as chairman and chief executive officer of SunGard Data Systems Inc. from 1986 to 2002 and remains the company's chairman. SunGard is one of the country's 15 largest computer services and software firms. A graduate of Wichita State University, Mann served as a pilot in the air force after graduation. He has been an executive and entrepreneur in the computer services industry since 1960.

My interest in computer technology and the desire to be in charge of my own company compelled me to leave IBM three years later to join Fox and Company, a smaller company in my hometown of Wichita, Kansas. They had acquired an early computer software and service business and hired me, at age 29, to run it.

As my experience with computers grew, I also gained insight into how to run a company, which would prove to be very valuable as I continued through my career. I learned that to be successful you have to have a successful product, and I was able to design and develop one of the four early computer income tax preparation programs. This turned out to be very profitable.

The company's decision to merge with four similar small companies from around the country, however, was a different matter. We later learned all except mine were losing money, and the company collapsed—putting me in the challenging position of trying to turn a company around for the first time.

That struggle taught me that you cannot spend

> Embrace your mistakes—there's plenty to learn from them.

more money than you are taking in. Throughout my career, I never forgot this experience.

Another quality that served me well was one that I learned from my father, who had been an insurance salesman for most of his life. He had the ability to negotiate with people instead of getting drawn into arguments by them—disagreeing agreeably, if you will. Even though I got into many contentious situations, I was always able to turn those disagreements into positive negotiations thanks to his example.

You've also got to embrace your mistakes—there's plenty to be learned from them as well. For example, I had gone to college at Wichita State with the founders of Pizza Hut, and obviously their company turned out to be extremely successful. So I decided I wanted to get into the business as well, but by that time all of the Pizza Hut franchises had been awarded. I asked my friend what other company he would recommend, and he said Godfather's Pizza.

I took my profits from the computer company and opened five Godfather's franchises in Wisconsin. They bombed, and I lost my original investment and more—but I took a couple of things away from this experience, too. First, I realized this line of work was not for me, and, second, I learned the hard way not to allow myself to be distracted by fads and trends.

The key to success in any business is to keep your head down and just use common-sense business fundamentals. You have to find out how your company can make money, and then how to increase it every year. Any business is going to have setbacks, so you just have to learn from them and be able to overcome them.

After the Godfather's flop, I was able to help form SunGard Data Systems, a company that primarily has two lines of business: availability services and computer center disaster recovery services.

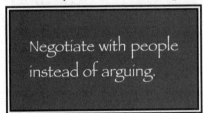

Negotiate with people instead of arguing.

Both of these lines have been extremely successful.

Since 1983, when it was formed, the corporation's revenue has grown from $30 million to $3.6 billion. We have four principles that we try to follow, which I think are keys to any successful business: strategic prudence, management precision, professional excellence and performance rewards.

I never had a drastic epiphany or saw any bright lights that directed my career down a certain path, but I was always lucky enough to be in the right place at the right time. Forty years ago, I had no idea how much our world would come to be dominated by computers. I believed that their acceptance was inevitable because they made it so much easier to do things, but I did not envision virtually everyone I know having multiple computers doing their daily tasks.

BERNARD MARCUS

Being fired from a job is never a pleasant experience, but as I look back on my career, I can honestly say that it was the best thing that ever happened to me.

My first goal in life had been to become a doctor, a dream I failed to realize because our family did not have the money to pay the tuition. I worked at a grocery store after school doing a variety of jobs. The owner was a Russian immigrant, like my parents, and he was the first person who taught me the customer was "gold." Money was so critical that 10 cents was very important to him.

It was interesting to watch how he dealt with overstock, selling products that many times his customers did not want, and making sure he had the products the customer did want. The lessons I learned from him stayed with me the rest of my life.

After school I went to work as a pharmacist. That early in my career, however, I knew I was more comfortable dealing with customers than working on processes. I preferred to come out from behind the counter to sell and communicate with the customers, rather than to stay back with my partner and compound prescriptions.

I soon realized retail was in my blood.

I moved over to general retailing, working for a company called Two Guys, in New Jersey. This experience broadened my

BERNARD MARCUS is co-founder of The Home Depot, Inc., the world's largest home improvement retailer. He served as chairman of the board until his retirement in 2002. From 1972 to 1978, Marcus was chairman of the board and president of The Handy Dan Improvement Centers, Inc. A graduate of Rutgers University, Marcus and his wife, Billi, established The Marcus Institute in 1991 and The Marcus Foundation to further his desire to give back to the community. A centerpiece of his civic involvement is the $200 million Georgia Aquarium, now under construction in Atlanta. It will be the largest aquarium in the United States and one of the largest in the world when it opens in 2005.

outlook. Two Guys was a forerunner of the Wal-Mart Supercenter. I left there to work for the Odell Co., selling products to a variety of stores, and went from there to Handy Dan in the mid-1970s.

I was fired as the chief executive officer of Handy Dan in 1978, which set the stage for me to create The Home Depot. If I had stayed at Handy Dan, I would have been successful, but I would not have been able to revolutionize the home improvement industry.

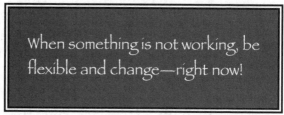

When something is not working, be flexible and change—right now!

A group of investors believed in what I wanted to do, and we put together a team that opened four stores in the Atlanta area in 1979, two on the same day and two about four months later. It took about a year to get them going. The first two stores really struggled but slowly started to catch on, and then the business became a roaring success. Today, just 25 years after we opened those first stores, there are 1,750 Home Depot outlets.

It was the right place at the right time with the right philosophy—that's why Home Depot has become such a success. We surrounded ourselves with good people and we believed in them. We sought out people who were entrepreneurial. We hired workers who were better equipped and smarter than we were.

Most businesses start with good team members but cannot foster the proper environment for them to grow. It is important to allow people to be active team members and not force them to be mirror images of yourself.

Communication is paramount to the success of a business. If people don't understand what you are trying to do, they can't strive to meet your goals. I have found through my experiences that communication is not only speaking—it also involves listening. And when you listen, keep an open mind. I've always tried to keep my mouth closed and my ears open. I've learned a great deal from unconventional sources, such as clerks, customers, and so on.

Another reason for our success is that we didn't set our goals too high. They were not easily reached, but they were achievable.

This allowed us to build a company with high enthusiasm, a great culture and outstanding results.

The vibrancy of the retail business, having the right products, knowing how to display them, knowing the customers, knowing how to gain loyalty from the customers, knowing my associates and how to motivate them—these became the standard tools of my professional life.

Another valuable lesson I've learned over the years is that you have to be able to realize when something you are doing is not working—and to be flexible enough to change. Every bad decision you make should teach you something that will help make you stronger. You also have to realize you will have critics, people won't always agree with everything you are doing—and you have to be able to weath-er the down

Always listen and keep an open mind.

times and not let the storms destroy you.

Our best advice, though, has come from our customers—they've basically told us what to do. It was a lesson I learned from my boss at the grocery store many years ago—listen to your customers and treat each of them like they're the most important person in the world. That has been the basic reason for our success.

CHARLES PETER McCOLOUGH

I was a seventh-grade student in my hometown of Halifax, Nova Scotia, when I met a woman who expanded my horizons and taught me there was a much bigger and more interesting world beyond the borders of my hometown.

Her name was Blanche Meagher, and for three years, she was my teacher. She talked a lot about the world, its people and politics. Her favorite topic was the League of Nations, and she eventually left the teaching profession to enter the Canadian Diplomat Service and went on to become Canada's first female ambassador.

I went on to serve in the British Navy during World War II, and afterward I attended law school in Toronto and then moved to the United States to attend the Harvard Business School. I wanted to obtain some sales experience, so I went to work for a chemical company, knowing I wouldn't be staying there long.

One of my friends from Harvard was living in Philadelphia, and I went to visit him for the weekend. He happened to have an interview with an executive search firm, so I tagged along and asked the recruiter to also look at my resume.

It turned out the president of the company that had retained the recruiting company was a lawyer and was looking for someone with both a legal and sales background. I got the job offer and my friend didn't.

C. PETER MCCOLOUGH is the former chairman and CEO of the Xerox Corporation. He joined the firm in 1954, when it was known as the Haloid Co., a manufacturer of industrial photographic products. Five years later the company introduced the first office copying machine. McColough took over as the firm's president in 1966.

I was working for that company when I got an invitation to interview with the Haloid Company in Rochester, New York. It was a small, family-controlled photographic company of modest size and success. I wasn't particularly interested in moving to upstate New York or to that company, so I delayed my visit until a work-related trip took me there.

Although I was not impressed with their new technology, called xerography, I was tremendously impressed with the company's founder, Joseph C. Wilson, with whom I talked for several hours. I liked what he hoped to do with the technology, but more importantly I liked his sense of responsibility to his employees, stockholders and Rochester. He did not make me a job offer that day, but I left that meeting convinced I would accept an offer if one came at a later date.

In fact, an offer came soon thereafter, and I said yes. It was then that my business education really began. Almost everything I learned as a manager came from Joe Wilson. He taught me to set the horizon at a healthy distance in the development of any new technology. Time after time he said to me, "Most people exaggerate what they can do in the short run for

> Long-term success has to be the goal—not short-term results.

their own development or that of their company, but also grossly underestimate what they can do in the long run if they put their heads and minds to that end."

At the time, the company was trying to develop technology and materials for duplicating machines. Joe was convinced the technology could be refined into making copiers less labor-intensive and more productive.

It really took him, and us, about 20 years to do it, but he was right. The company, which eventually changed its name to Xerox, became very successful. I received added responsibilities each year because Joe had decided that he wanted me to succeed him as the chief executive officer when he retired in 1968, and that really broadened my scope and understanding of the business.

I tried to follow his example and his philosophy of business, especially his view that the long-term success and plan for a company is much more important than its short-term results. It definitely worked for our company. We always had a strictly detailed five-year plan that we followed, and we never wavered from it.

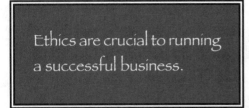

Ethics are crucial to running a successful business.

The other advice Joe gave me, which I always thought was important, was that ethics are highly important to the success of any business. I am really horrified by what I see happening in the financial world today with all of the crookedness and lack of ethics.

As executives, we never expected to make the kind of money we made, but that wasn't our primary incentive. It was more important to us to create a product of value, something of which we could be proud. We also knew that if we did that, everything else would take care of itself.

ROBERT S. MILLER

I had been working in the finance office of Ford Motor Company for 11 years, eight of those years in Mexico City, Melbourne, Australia, and Caracas, Venezuela, when Lee Iacocca was fired from his position of president at Ford. He soon found himself at Chrysler, which was in the midst of a debt crisis and about to go out of business.

Iacocca began hiring people away from Ford, and he invited me to join the effort to save Chrysler. I was not wild about the idea—many people doubted Chrysler would be in business long enough to pay my moving bills. The company's only prospect for recovery was at the mercy of Congress.

There has never been a salesman like Iacocca, however. After an hour in his office, I was ready to go back to Caracas, pack my bags and report to work at my new place of employment on Monday morning. It was only after I left that I realized we had never talked about my salary.

It was hard to walk away from Ford, where I had been working since graduating from the Harvard Law School and having earned an MBA from Stanford. (I had flunked the Oregon bar exam, but that was fine by me, because I really hated law school and didn't want to be a lawyer anyway.)

ROBERT STEVE MILLER spent 23 years in the automobile industry, first at Ford Motor Company and then at Chrysler, where he served as chief financial officer and later as vice chairman. He also has worked in investment banking and as "professional corporate director." Eight times in the past decade he has returned to active duty as a full-time executive. Miller lives with his wife, Maggie, in Sunriver, Oregon, where his numerous hobbies include skiing and model railroading.

As difficult as it was to leave Ford, I thought the challenge of trying to keep Chrysler in business was a higher calling. We estimated that 500,000 American jobs might be irretrievably lost if Chrysler went out of business. I woke up many times at four in the morning in a cold sweat, realizing that if I made a mistake that day it could end up jeopardizing the livelihood of half a million American families.

My first week consisted of several all-night sessions and the ever-present thought of what I had gotten myself into. I was 38 years old, and it was my job to negotiate the terms of Chrysler's survival with banks, labor unions, foreign governments and thousands of suppliers.

To qualify for government loan guarantees, we needed the unanimous approval of concessions from all of Chrysler's 400 banks around the world. It took nine months to complete all of the negotiations, and we are always teetering on the verge of collapse. Ironically, the bank with the longest overdue loan was the first bank to sign the Chrysler deal.

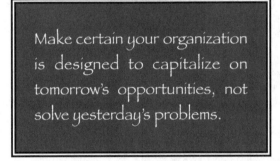

Make certain your organization is designed to capitalize on tomorrow's opportunities, not solve yesterday's problems.

It was my home state bank, the First Interstate Bank of Oregon. I called one of the directors to express my appreciation of their support.

When he picked up, I simply said, "Thanks, Dad."

We finally reached agreements with all of the banks but one, a small bank near one of our plants in Rockford, Illinois, that refused to extend our loan. The Chrysler saga was national news, and I went on television to point out that Chrysler would shut down and go out of business within days if this one bank would not agree to the deal.

The citizens of Rockford got into the act by withdrawing their money from the bank. Kids began picketing the bank with signs that read "Save my Daddy's job." The bank president even received bomb threats by phone. He finally had enough and signed the agreement.

Then came the enormous task of signing more than 10,000 documents that had been accumulated by the more than 50 law firms working on the case. We got all of the papers assembled in offices on the 35th floor of a building on Park Avenue in New York. We had just begun signing the papers when I looked out the window and saw clouds of black smoke—there was a fire raging on the 20th floor of our building.

We hurried down the 35 flights of stairs to safety, reaching the outside as huge four-foot by eight-foot sheets of glass were exploding out of the building and crashing all around us. I took this as a sign from God to forget the government bailout and stop messing with the free enterprise system.

At midnight we were allowed back into the building, and found all of the documents were safe. By mid-morning everything was signed, and we had a historic closing. I took the half-billion dollar check that saved Chrysler and walked across the street and deposited it at an ordinary teller's window. I still have the receipt.

Completing the negotiations and receiving the bailout money was a good start, but it did not mean the turnaround was assured. Key elements included visible leadership, decisive action, dramatic cost cutting and upgrading of products and product quality. Iacocca was a

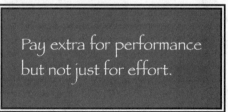

Pay extra for performance but not just for effort.

great leader because he could pick a priority and relentlessly pursue it. One of the biggest problems facing Chrysler in 1980 was an embarrassing frequency of product defects, which was driving away customers.

Iacocca decided we should extend our warranties from 12 months to five years, an industry blockbuster at the time. I told him the idea was crazy, and so did others. I thought we would go broke on the warranty bills. The manufacturing and marketing departments also were against it, but Iacocca was adamant. His reasoning was that if quality didn't improve, we'd be out of business, and then all of the other objectives would not matter anyway.

Of course he was right. Extending the warranty forced Chrysler to build cars that would last for years instead of falling apart. Iacocca went a further step by imposing a bonus system that paid zero to every executive in any year that quality didn't improve by a targeted amount. Defect rates were reduced over time by 90 percent.

Working for Iacocca was a great privilege. I accompanied him on a trip to Japan and South Korea, where he was greeted by cheering crowds. Actually, they were cheering me when we arrived in Seoul because I was riding in a big limo and he was in a nondescript grey Chrysler. When I asked him about it later, he said that was for security reasons. If there had been trouble, guess who would have been shot?

I ended up staying at Chrysler for a dozen years before launching into a career that has seen me help perform similar turnaround challenges with many other companies, including Waste Management, Bethlehem Steel and Federal Mogul. Along the way I have learned a few lessons that were common to all of those companies.

Working with so many businesses under stress has taught me that there are many great people working for those companies— they just need that decisive and quality leadership to be successful. Such businesses also listen to the customer and are well organized.

My best advice for young people beginning their business careers is to tell the truth. I would be a terrible poker player because I can't lie. I have also found that it doesn't make any difference what you select early on as a career "path." Do what sounds like fun. Don't do something just because it is in vogue or happens to be the so-called fast track. Do what you love to do and your passion is bound to make you successful.

THOMAS S. MURPHY

The most important break in my business career happened because I remembered a story my father had told me when I was growing up.

My father, Charles Murphy, had a varied business background before going to law school at night. He worked in the asphalt department at Texaco and as a lawyer who represented many advertising clients. He was also president of the Advertising Club of New York.

One day, my father was having a conversation with a business friend, who was the head of Conoco Oil. He told my father he was looking for someone to be the general counsel of his company and the head of the advertising department. He suggested that he was hoping to find an individual with a background in the oil business and that, if he turned out to be a good employee, this person would have a good chance at becoming the next CEO of the company.

My father replied that it would be hard to find someone with that kind of background, but he would think about it and let his friend know if someone came to mind. Someone eventually did, and that person got the job and went on to become president of Conoco.

Years later, when they met again, my father's friend asked him, "Charlie, why didn't you take the job I offered you?"

THOMAS S. MURPHY is chairman and chief executive officer emeritus of Capital Cities/ABC Inc. ABC Inc. is an indirect subsidiary of The Walt Disney Co., and Murphy is a member of The Walt Disney Company's board of directors. Murphy was chairman and CEO of Capital Cities/ABC from 1966 to 1990 and from 1994 to 1996. Murphy joined Capital Cities when it was founded in 1954 with one UHF television station and one radio station.

It had never occurred to my father that his friend had described to him all of those job requirements as a way to offer him the job.

I never forgot that story, and I know it was the only reason I was able to recognize a similar situation when it happened to me.

I was 29 years old when I accompanied my parents to a party at the home of Lowell Thomas, the great radio broadcaster, in Pauling, New York, on Labor Day weekend in 1954. At the party I was chatting with Frank Smith, who was Thomas's business manager. Frank was a friend and occasional golfing partner of my father. He knew I worked for Kenyon and Eckhart, an advertising agency, and Lever Bros., a major package goods company, and that I had graduated from the Harvard Business School.

Frank told me he was involved with a group of investors who were taking over a small UHF television station in Albany, New York—a little "crap shoot," he called it. He said, "Tom, you may know someone who might be interested in taking over a job as general manager of this station." Frank said they were looking for someone with a business background, the ability to be a good manager and knowledge of the advertising and package goods businesses.

My answer was basically the same as the one my father had given to his friend: I would think about it and get back to him if I thought of someone.

Later that afternoon, I was driving the 70 miles back to New York with my parents when I realized that Frank was offering the job to me. Being as square as my father, I would have completely missed that fact had I not remembered his experience years earlier.

So I went to work as the general manager of WROW-TV, Channel 41, in Albany on November 7, 1954. The company started out with the name Hudson Valley Broadcasting and an investment of just over $1 million. It was the best thing that ever happened to me. What it really gave me was the chance to run something, to see if I could do it.

I never had an unhappy day after that.

I stayed at the station for six years, during which time our company had purchased two additional stations. I then moved to New York to take over the operations of all three stations. We changed the name of the company to Capital Cities Broadcasting. The company continued to grow, thanks to Frank's leadership. He was very smart—to this day, one of the pieces of advice I try to give young people is to go to work for the smartest guy you can find who will hire you, and hope he teaches you the business.

By the time I was 40 or so I had been promoted to president and CEO and the company was prospering. I'd like to say I was smart enough to get into the television business just as it was beginning to grow, but really I took the job in Albany simply because it gave me the chance to run something. I was fortunate to have a boss who let me run the station and who hardly ever came to Albany, and that gave me great experience.

The company's name changed again in 1986, when we purchased the American Broadcasting Company for $3.5 billion. Ten years later, in 1996, Capital Cities/ABC was sold to the Walt Disney Company for $19 billion.

There is no question that it takes a lot of luck to be successful in corporate life, and it turned out I was in the right business at the right time. I enjoyed what I was doing, however, and there is no substitute for that. Young people need to find something they really like if they are going to be successful. I was able to do that, and to connect with a great boss.

My advice to corporate executives is almost the same as it is to young professionals, only in reverse. When they are looking for new employees, they should try to hire the smartest people they can find and not hire more than they need. The mission statement we included in our annual report at Cap Cities read: "Our goal is to hire the best people we can find and give them the responsibility and authority they need to perform their jobs."

What we always tried to do as a company was to follow the credo established by Johnson & Johnson years ago: Put the customers first. It worked well for them, and it worked for us. My own talents were pretty narrow, but what I think I did have was common sense—and that's pretty uncommon in corporate America, in my opinion.

DAVID NEELEMAN

It is natural for people to think that, because my career has been spent working in the airline and tourism industry, I must have fallen in love with airplanes and flying at an early age. Really, that was not the way it happened.

One day, when I was a student at the University of Utah, a girl who sat behind me in an accounting class told me about how her uncle had some time-share condos in Hawaii that he was having trouble renting. I really don't know why she told me that. For some reason, she asked if I would help him out, and I agreed to do it.

That was my introduction to the travel business.

I became a tour operator, but when the company went bankrupt, I didn't want anything more to do with the travel business. I was planning on going back to school when June Morris, who owned Morris Travel in Salt Lake City, began calling me. She wanted me to come and work for her company, running the same kind of tour agency.

I didn't call her back until one day when my uncle, who happened to be her attorney, called me and said, "Call her back and go see her. At least listen to what she has to say." I did—and she charmed me, so I went to work for her.

DAVID NEELEMAN is chairman and CEO of JetBlue Airways, which began operations in 2000 from its base at New York's John F. Kennedy Airport. It now serves 27 cities across the United States with a fleet of 61 planes. JetBlue is Neeleman's third successful aviation business. He founded Morris Air, a regional carrier that he sold to Southwest Airlines. He also started WestJet Airlines in Canada and implemented the industry's first electronic ticketing system. Neeleman and his wife, Vicki, are the parents of nine children and live in New Canaan, Connecticut.

I was 24 years old, and June put me on her board of directors and allowed me to buy some of the company. We started out as a charter operator with one airplane and that evolved into Morris Air Service, a regional airline, which became successful enough that we were able to sell it to Southwest Airlines.

The sale called for me to go to work for Southwest under a transition plan that was scheduled to last for a couple of years. After only a few months, however, I could see it wasn't going to work. I was driving them crazy, and they were driving me crazy. They were not perfect. I felt they were content to do business the way they had been doing it, and I thought there were a lot of things they could be doing better—I was really wearing on them.

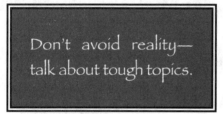

Don't avoid reality— talk about tough topics.

After five months, I was fired—but that was probably my one big break. If I had not been fired, I would never have started JetBlue.

Owning your own company allows you to do what you want to do, and when you start from the beginning, you can bring in your own people. That was what we did, and it has worked out extremely well.

In July 1999, we announced the new airline, and we began flying in 2000. We had a great management team in place and $130 million in capital funding from investors who believed we could turn into reality our mantra: Bringing humanity back to air travel.

The first flight was on February 11, 2000 between John F. Kennedy airport in New York and Fort Lauderdale, Florida. We now have 60 airplanes serving 24 cities with expansion planned that will have 305 airplanes flying to many more destinations by the year 2011.

We offer 24 channels of live satellite television free at every seat. We were the first U.S. airline to be 100 percent ticketless, the first to install bullet-proof cockpit doors across our fleet, and the first to install security cameras in passenger cabins.

Like all airlines, we faced a major challenge after the September 11, 2001, terrorist attacks in regaining the faith of our customers that they would be safe when they stepped on our planes. We tried to turn the negatives into a positive, and six weeks after the attacks, all of our planes were equipped with the bullet-proof cockpit doors. I knew I no longer wanted to fly on a plane that didn't provide that level of security, and I didn't think our customers would either.

We had our share of critics who said our airline would not be successful. They said we would not be able to offer low fares and still have great employees and provide great service to our customers. Twenty-two million customers later, maybe we have proven those critics wrong.

A major key to our company's success has been that we encourage all of our employees to do the best job they can do. If you take care of the people around you, generally things will work out pretty well.

One of the parts of my job I like the best is getting out and talking to the people who fly with us, finding out what they like about our airline and what they think we can do better. Every week I am on one of our planes flying somewhere, hanging out with the crew, helping to serve snacks, talking with the employees and the passengers. I can't stand to be in an office or in meetings all day.

As I talk to everyone, the most surprising thing to me about our airline is the loyalty of our customers. People really love flying JetBlue, and they are telling their friends about us. They truly are our best advertising, and that is very rewarding.

Mediocrity is pretty rampant in the customer service business these days, and I really don't think there are very many companies that people dream about doing business with. It's a shame, but these companies have forgotten the golden rule: You should make your best effort to treat everybody—employees and customers alike—the way you would like to be treated.

THOMAS J. NEFF

The middle of a recession might not seem like the best time to decide to switch careers. That was exactly what I did, however, and it has worked out extremely well.

I was 37 years old in 1974 and had spent three years working at TWA, where one of my job perks was a free first-class pass to anywhere in the world. As nice as that was, there seemed to be something missing. So, with the encouragement of friends, I decided to join the executive search profession.

It was an emerging field, but the recession had caused the search industry to shrink. Various firms had approached me over the previous eight years with offers to join their companies and I had resisted, believing the timing or the situation wasn't quite right.

I was actually in the planning stages of opening my own firm with a friend when I learned that one of the senior officers at Booz, Allen & Hamilton, one of the pioneer companies in the search business, had suffered a heart attack and was not able to continue to work. They asked me to replace him, and it provided me with a great opportunity to learn the business.

The goals of an executive search firm are the same as any company looking to hire a new corporate officer or a member of its board of directors. You want to find the best candidate for the job,

THOMAS J. NEFF has been the chairman, U.S., of Spencer Stuart since 1996 after serving as president of the company from 1979 to 1996. He joined Spencer Stuart in 1976 after working for three years at Booz, Allen & Hamilton, Inc. He previously worked for Hospital Data Sciences, Inc., TWA and McKinsey & Co. Neff is a graduate of Lafayette College and earned his MBA at Lehigh University. He is married and is the father of five children.

matching the company's needs with the individual's skills and talents.

Executive searches require a strong work ethic, high standards, a client-service orientation and an entrepreneurial bent. You have to be able to communicate well with people, build up a trust factor not only with the companies you are working for, but with the individual candidates.

The key to finding the right person for the right job is to understand both the needs of the company and the abilities of the individual. You can have a great company and a great individual, but the two don't necessarily match up correctly. You have to realize when matches won't work and prevent it from happening.

In looking back, I had been well prepared. My father was a great role model for me because he had a tremendous work ethic and was a creative thinker. I thought back on his advice often, as I also recalled my training in school, in the army and in my first corporate job, working for McKinsey & Co.

I was born into a traditional Irish-Catholic family, the youngest of five boys. We lived in Easton, Pennsylvania, and I was raised in the parochial school system. We had 24 students (boys and girls) in my graduating high school class, and the only sport available to us was basketball. We didn't even have our own gym.

Even though I was only about six feet tall, I played center, against much taller opponents, and during my junior year we actually completed an undefeated season and won our league championship. I enjoyed sports enormously, and I believe the love of competition, the teamwork and the desire for success that I learned at an early age has carried over to my experiences in the business world.

Being able to get along with others and succeed in a team environment is really no different in sports than it is in business. No one working alone is going to be successful. I once scored 56 points in a basketball game while I was in college, outscoring the opposition by myself, but I wouldn't have been able to do that without my teammates there to pass me the ball.

Another similarity between business and sports is that you cannot replace hard work. You don't have to be the smartest person in the world, just like you don't have to be the best player, but you have to know how to get your job done. You have to be able to deliver results.

I had been working at Booz Allen for a couple of years when I was recruited by Spencer Stuart to run its New York office. I was in the right place at the right time a couple of years later when our firm's chairman, a distinguished Englishman, was tapped by newly elected Prime Minister Margaret Thatcher to join her new cabinet. I was named president and managing partner (CEO) of Spencer Stuart.

In the eight years I was in that position, Spencer Stuart's global revenues quadrupled. We doubled the number of offices around the world. I left that position after my first wife died in 1985, but I have continued to enjoy great success with clients and as the chairman of U.S. operations.

We always follow up after we place someone in a new position, because the keys to our company's success are helping clients select the right person for the job and helping to ensure their continued success. Since 1985, I have conducted more than 100 CEO searches and 300 board of directors searches.

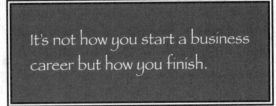

It's not how you start a business career but how you finish.

Most young people today don't realize when they take their first job that they will likely work for seven or eight different companies during their careers. It's very important to start out with a good organization, where you can get valuable mentoring and can learn the skills that are important to the company and transferable to other organizations.

Part of the reason for the success I have achieved has been that I have a true passion for what I am doing. Success also comes from being able to work with good people whom you enjoy. You also have to be fortunate enough to work for a great organization.

DAVID NOVAK

My biggest break was showing up on this earth as the son of Charles and Jean Novak.

My father worked for the Coast and Geodetic Survey. He served on a survey team that established the latitude and longitude points for map making. As a result, I had gone to three different schools a year and lived in 23 states by the time I was in the seventh grade. I was born in Beeville, Texas, a tiny little town outside of San Antonio, and some of the towns we moved to after that were Chama, New Mexico, Detroit Lakes, Minnesota, and Dodge City, Kansas—twice.

The largest home we ever had was an eight-foot by 40-foot trailer. When it was time to move to the next town, we simply hooked Dad's government truck up to the trailer and hauled it on down the road. Each time my Mom would take me to a new school, and she would say, "You'd better take the first step to make friends, because if you wait, before you know it we'll be on our way and you won't have had as much fun as you should." Her advice and these experiences taught me how to quickly size up new situations, read people and make friends.

My dad taught me how to coach simply by being a great one himself. He managed my Little League teams and always took pride in developing the skills of kids with a wide range of talents.

DAVID C. NOVAK is the chairman, CEO and president of Yum! Brands Inc., the world's largest restaurant company, with more than 33,000 restaurants in over 100 countries and territories. It is the parent company to A&W All-American Food, KFC, Long John Silver's, Pizza Hut, and Taco Bell. Novak held senior management positions in marketing and operations at Pepsi Cola Co. for 20 years, and was president of both KFC and Pizza Hut. Novak lives in Anchorage, Kentucky, with his wife, Wendy.

I happened to be a fairly good player, and he pointed out ways I could do even better. He taught me, in a motivational way, how to raise the bar on performance.

Both of my parents taught me the value of hard work. They rolled up their sleeves and worked diligently in everything they did, and if it wasn't done right, they would keep at it until it was. Their number-one goal was to raise their kids in a way that would give them the best opportunity to succeed in life. Their formal education stopped after high school, but they made certain that I had the means to go to college. When I graduated from the University of Missouri, I became the first man in my dad's family to earn a college degree. They wanted me to live the American dream, and I have. A lot of kids with similar backgrounds haven't had the good fortune I've had. My parents made the difference. Their love and the values they instilled, along with God's grace, represent the foundation of any success I have had.

The second (in sequential order only, so I don't get in trouble at home) biggest break I had was marrying Wendy, my wife of 30 years. She is beautiful inside and out and has been a constant source of encouragement for me. She has an almost uncanny ability to tell it like it is and can always set me straight on any issue. Wendy has a way of helping me to see any situation for what it really is, rather than seeing it as I would like it to be. She is a great judge of people, and I make certain she meets every major recruit before I extend them a job offer—the one time I didn't, she met the guy after I had hired him and told me he would never make it. Sadly, she was right.

Wendy is also a source of inspiration to me because of her courage. Having been a juvenile diabetic, she once told me she would never be able to have kids. Nine years into our marriage, though, she decided she wanted to give it a try. Our daughter, Ashley, was born 10 weeks premature, survived Hylands Membrane disease and is now attacking life as a healthy, vibrant 22-year-old. Unfortunately, the effects of the pregnancy led to temporary blindness and severe eye complications for Wendy. She has weathered it all without complaint and with a positive attitude. I've seen a lot of men go down the tubes because they didn't have the right partner in life. Wendy is exactly the partner I've needed.

On the career front, everyone needs to be taught, and I've been coached by the best. All of them either went on to run a function in a large company or be chairman and CEO. Tom James went on to be the senior vice president of marketing for Pizza Hut. Howard Davis went on to be Chairman and CEO of Tracy-Locke Advertising. Steve Reinemund went on to be chairman and CEO of PepsiCo, Craig Weatherup went on to be chairman and CEO of Pepsi Bottling Group and Roger Enrico went on to be chairman and CEO of PepsiCo. You would have to be considered lucky to work for just one of these great leaders—and I worked for all of them. All of them gave me the feedback and support I needed to climb the ranks.

The best teacher of them all was Andy Pearson, the founding chairman of the company I now head. Andy and I partnered up when Pizza Hut, Taco Bell and KFC were spun off from PepsiCo. Andy is the youngest 78-year-old I've ever seen and an insatiable learner. I consider myself fortunate that he has passed his knowledge and wisdom on to me. I still talk to Andy once or twice a week to get his insight and advice. I've sponged off his experience consulting at McKinsey, running PepsiCo, teaching at Harvard and buying companies at Clayton, Dubilier and Rice. How many guys get an opportunity like that?

It seems I have always been in the right place at the right time. I was president of both Pizza Hut and KFC when the companies were spun off from PepsiCo. Roger Enrico made me vice chairman and president of the new venture. I've had the opportunity to build a company that I love and that does business in 100 countries. We have created a high-energy, people-first, customer-mania culture that is centered on a spirited recognition of capability that drives performance. In so doing, we have more than tripled our earnings per share and market capitalization in a little more than six years. To think, at one time, I saw myself as a PepsiCo lifer and wouldn't have been able to fathom what has since happened to me.

One credo I have always believed in more than anything is that leadership is a privilege. A lot of people have talent and work hard, but not everyone gets the top job. I honestly believe both my parents could have run companies if they had received the same breaks I have received. I remember the day, when I was the head of marketing for Pizza Hut, that I introduced my dad to Steve Reinemund, the Pizza Hut president. My Dad addressed him as "Mr. Reinemund." That puzzled me because he was more than 20 years older than Steve, so later I asked him why he had done that. He simply replied, "Because he's the president."

In our company, we stress that everyone—regardless of their position—can lead and make a difference. One of my mottos is, "Don't look up, don't look down, always look straight ahead." One of our internal battle cries is for everybody to "be the leader, act like the leader."

The most powerful way I have executed the privilege of leadership is through recognition. When I was chief operating officer for Pepsi Cola Co., I always conducted 6:00 a.m. round-table discussions with the route salesmen to see what was really happening on the front line. One day, when I asked a question about merchandising, everyone at the

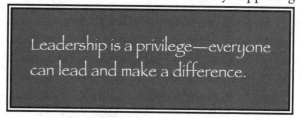

Leadership is a privilege—everyone can lead and make a difference.

table started raving about Bob and how good he was at his job. Bob started crying. When I asked him why, he replied, "I've been in this company for 42 years and I never knew people felt this way about me." Then and there I vowed to myself to make recognition a major pillar of the work I did from that point forward.

When I became president of KFC, I began spontaneously giving out floppy rubber chickens—along with a $100 bill (because you can't eat a rubber chicken)—when I saw great performances. Grown men and women cried when I did it. When I moved over to Pizza Hut, I gave away Green Bay Packer cheesehead hats. Now, as the chairman and CEO of Yum! Brands, I give away wind-up smiling teeth to our team members for putting a "yum!" on the faces of our customers.

We have made employee recognition a big part of our companies. All of the leaders of Yum! Brands now have their own individual recognition award. A franchisee in Arkansas gives out a pig helmet for his Razorback award. In Thailand, the president of our operation there gives out a deck of cards with his picture as the king. When I go to China, the president gives out a dragon award. People like to be appreciated. It makes them feel like they are important and what they do is relevant. Recognizing others and watching others learn the power of recognition has given me incredible joy.

Another component in a company's success is a leader who takes the time to listen to and ask questions of the people who work there. The people who work closest to the customer are the ones who know what is going on. You have to go to the front line if you want to find out what customers are saying, and then you have to make sure you respond.

One of my observations over the years has been that the people who are the most successful are the ones who are passionate about their job, who have positive energy and who are smart. What separates them from the rest is their desire to be an avid learner. When you talk to people you have to ask questions.

You can learn something from everybody.

FRANK A. OLSON

In 1950, I was a freshman at San Francisco State and the Korean War loomed on the horizon. A friend and classmate of mine was working as a part-time car rental agent at the San Francisco airport when he got the news that he had been drafted into the army. He told me that as result, his job would soon be available, so I went to the airport and applied.

I had no idea that such a casual conversation would launch me into an unbelievable career.

I got the job. At the time, that was really all I thought it was—a job—and I was glad to have it. I didn't have any real objective other than to do the job as well as I possibly could. Two years later, due to financial reasons, I opted to become a full-time employee and to continue my education by attending night school, taking three classes a semester.

Five brothers owned the company, which was a local one, and they had the exclusive franchise for the transportation of passengers at the airport. They had the car rental agency and also owned the airport bus company.

Over the years I continued to earn additional responsibilities, and at the age of 24 or 25 I was appointed supervisor in charge of operations of the bus company. When I was 30, one brother

FRANK OLSON is the chairman of the board of The Hertz Corporation, having joined the company as a vice president of a Hertz subsidiary in San Francisco in 1964. A graduate of City College in San Francisco, Olson was elected president and CEO of Hertz in 1977. He also served as the executive vice president of RCA Corporation and as chairman and CEO of Allegis Corp., both parent companies of Hertz.

bought out the others and named me general manager of all of the operations at the airport.

This gave me tremendous experience: I was involved in labor relations, financing, sales, marketing, capital planning, budgeting, every aspect of running the business. It was quite an education.

In 1964, I was recruited to join the Hertz car rental company in New York. By this time I had graduated from college and had realized that I wanted to pursue my career in that business. Hertz was the largest car rental company in the world, and I thought the offer held great potential.

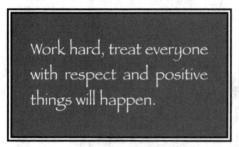

Work hard, treat everyone with respect and positive things will happen.

It was the right decision, as all of my local experience had prepared me for the challenge of working for a national company. I never aspired to another job, never looked for the next job. I was devoted to doing the best that I possibly could at the job I had. Over the years I supervised a lot of young people and saw how many of them had their sights set on a certain position. It most cases I don't think they ever got it, because they were worried more about trying to get that job than doing the one they had.

I always wanted to take on as much responsibility as I could. I wanted to challenge myself to see if I could do it. Whenever I was asked to take on another job I wouldn't hesitate to reply, "Yes, I can do it."

Business is all about competition, but it also has to be fun. It's not just a question of money. Too many young people don't realize that. The competition excited me. I wanted to find out where the bar was where I could no longer outperform my competitors. You have to surround yourself with people who have fire in their bellies and want to win. If you do that, you can't lose.

When I became CEO at Hertz in 1977, the company's sales were $400 million with profits of $60 million a year. When I retired, sales were $5 billion and profits $600 million a year.

Hertz was acquired by RCA in 1967. Three years later, I was promoted to vice president and general manager for Hertz's U.S. operations. In 1977, I was elected president and chief executive officer for Hertz.

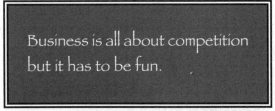

Business is all about competition but it has to be fun.

In 1980, I was appointed executive vice president in charge of all of RCA's diversified businesses, including C.I.T., Coronet Carpets, Banquet Foods, Oriel Foods and RCA Records. This position exposed me to the businesses of finance, manufacturing and entertainment, among others.

In 1985, United Airlines bought Hertz and I returned to the company as CEO. I later also became the chairman of United, Westin and Hilton Hotels. The company sold off Westin and Hilton, and I asked to return to my roots at Hertz. I retired in 2000 after 35 years at Hertz and remained as non-executive chairman until 2003.

My credo in life and business has been to do the best I could at whatever position I've had. I never had a goal of another position. I've simply believed that, if you work hard and treat everyone with respect, things will develop in a positive way.

ANDRALL E. PEARSON

I was working as a management consultant at McKinsey & Co. in New York, my second job after college, when a stranger walked into our offices. His name was Herman Lay, and he wanted to know if we could help him decide whether his company should acquire Seapak, a small regional seafood company.

Lay, it turned out, owned a rapidly growing snack food company in Atlanta named the H.W. Lay Co. Under normal circumstances, McKinsey would not have been interested in such an arrangement, because the company was always looking more toward long-term relationships.

In this case, however, they decided to take on the assignment, purely as a training experience for me. It was a test to see if I could manage an acquisition study on my own at the relatively young age of 30. I was not particularly happy about the assignment, because I didn't think whatever I did for this smaller company would be valued as highly as the work performed for McKinsey's major clients.

When Lay and I talked, he told me his goals in acquiring the company were faster growth, diversification and the creation of a strong national frozen seafood brand. To Lay's surprise, I called him just three weeks later with the answers to his questions. Our study had determined acquiring the company would meet none of

During his more than 40 years as a business leader, *ANDRALL PEARSON* has been an executive with five major organizations: PepsiCo, Yum! Brands, Harvard Business School, McKinsey & Company and Clayton Dubilier & Rice. He was the CEO of Tricon Global Restaurants (now called Yum! Brands)—Pizza Hut, Taco Bell, KFC, Long John Silver's and A&W Restaurants—the largest restaurant chain in the world. He also spent 15 years as president and chief operating officer of PepsiCo. Pearson and his wife, Joanne, live in Greenwich, Connecticut, and Palm Beach, Florida. They are the parents of a daughter and have two grandchildren.

his requirements—its growth was erratic, the frozen seafood industry was not doing well, and there seemed to be no chance to make the company a national brand.

I recommended that we stop the study and not spend any more time or money. Lay agreed, and he expressed his gratitude and astonishment that a consultant would terminate a study that had been scheduled to run for several months. He told me that I would hear from him again.

Several years later, I did indeed hear from him again. He stopped by my office to ask if I could study whether it would make sense for him to merge H.W. Lay with The Frito Co. That study was also easy, and the merger of the two companies into Frito-Lay was a major success.

More time passed, and eventually Frito-Lay merged with Pepsi Cola into what became PepsiCo. Lay showed up in my office again—this time with his president, Donald Kendall. They wanted to know if PepsiCo should acquire Schaeffer Beer, a strong New York brewer. Their concept was to capitalize on Pepsi's beverage and marketing know-how and progressively build Schaeffer into a national brand that could challenge Budweiser and Miller.

About four weeks later, I called Kendall and Lay to set up a meeting to discuss the study. I recommended they drop the idea, believing the merger would not benefit PepsiCo. Lay and Kendall agreed, and Lay next asked me to study his old company, Frito-Lay. That study led to the creation of a more centralized Frito-Lay and an increase in the profits of a company I thought was already well managed.

My work over the years as a consultant for Lay and Kendall led them to offer me the job as president of PepsiCo., by then a $1 billion conglomerate. I spent the next 15 years running one of the most exciting and rapidly growing consumer goods companies in the world.

I had been at PepsiCo for 14 years when I was invited to be the keynote speaker at a Business Week conference in Canada. As part of the publicity for the conference, I was interviewed on the CBC television network about how to build a good company into a great company. It so happened that the dean of the Harvard

Business School, a native Canadian, was visiting Vancouver and saw the interview.

He contacted me and ultimately asked me to become a tenured professor at the Harvard Business School, largely because of the work I had done at PepsiCo., which was basically following the examples I had learned at Harvard and McKinsey & Co. I was 60 years old, and I was excited by the challenge.

At first, though, I was a little ill at ease at the thought of becoming a full professor at Harvard despite having never taught a single class in any subject at any scholastic institution—and it showed. On my second day of teaching, we were discussing the story of a frozen lobster company attempting to become a branded competitor. One of the key questions was whether the lobster company could command a premium price for a commodity. When the male student I called on couldn't answer the question, I turned to a female student and said, "Let's get a housewife's perspective." All of the women in the class gasped. I immediately knew I had made a mistake and quickly tried to apologize, but I wasn't certain how that was received.

> Tackle every challenge with passion and gusto—it may be your big break.

The next day, the class had a surprise for me. They set out a bottle of Pepsi and a bottle of Coca Cola and said, "We want you to take the Pepsi challenge." One of the students poured the sodas into two unmarked glasses and asked me to tell the class which was Pepsi, a fair amount of pressure for a rookie professor in front of 100 or more students. Luckily I passed the test, and the rest of the semester went by without incident.

What my career in business and my experience at Harvard taught me was to tackle every challenge you face as if it might be a big break. Even though the assignment might seem small, it could well have a huge impact on your career. Whatever you are asked to do, if you do it well—better than your bosses had expected—you will be noticed and recognized.

JOHN A. POWERS

My big break came in the spring of 1965. I had gotten into advertising quite by accident. Upon returning from the service to complete my college education, I had taken a summer job for a promotion company selling television and sports programs to local stations across the country. After graduation, those contacts led to a position with Marschalk and Pratt, prior to its merger with McCann-Erickson. I had then been promoted to an account executive position on the Esso Standard Oil account, where we developed the "Tiger in the Tank" program and took it worldwide in one of the industry's first global advertising campaigns.

Then, in 1965, I found myself sitting down to lunch with Marion Harper, the chairman at Interpublic. I suspected I had been invited for another discussion about the strategy plan I was completing as part of the planning group of the newly formed Interpublic Group of Companies.

Instead, I was presented with four opportunities. One led to success. They all might have, perhaps, but it was the choice that led me to define my path to success—not how I would get there, but why.

The four options Harper laid out for me during that lunch were: to run the Houston office, where Esso Standard Oil had

JOHN POWERS's business career spanned 42 years with two companies, the Interpublic Group of Companies and Heublein, Inc. He was president of McCann-Erickson Europe and president and chief operating officer of McCann-Erickson, Inc., before becoming chairman and CEO of United Vintners, Inc., a subsidiary of Heublein in 1973. He later became president and chief operating officer of Heublein. A native of New York, Powers graduated from St. Peter's College and the Harvard University Advanced Management Program. He and his wife, Eileen, live with their family in New York.

transferred; to become vice chairman of Interpublic Group in Geneva; to remain in New York as part of the Interpublic Group; or to move to London as chairman of McCann-Erickson UK.

That weekend I studied each option carefully, discussed them all with my wife, and tried to determine which course would be best for my career. On the surface, each offer seemed very disconnected from the others, presenting distinctly different challenges and growth opportunities. Over the course of the weekend, though, I came to realize that Houston, Geneva, New York and London were actually quite similar. The common denominator was that each office was experiencing some upheaval, fraught with either business or leadership problems, and needed to be guided to calmer waters as a condition for growth.

It was a singular moment—I realized what my role in business would be, what people expected from me, and where my strengths lay. Harper was a keen mentor who presented me with these opportunities because he had recognized my strengths even before I did.

He had identified me as a fixer.

As I looked back on my career up to that point, I saw that I had always relished the chance to fix a problem, and the challenge of finding a better way inspired and motivated me. I've since learned that those who are willing to lead the charge, to go head-first into a battle, create an energy that can be inspirational and contagious. Harper had the wisdom to zero in not only on my strength as an individual, but also on my value to those with whom I worked.

Serving as a company commander in Korea following the end of World War II had lain the groundwork for these strengths. At 19, my military responsibilities forced an understanding of accountability, leadership, and unflinching determination. It was quite simple—you were respected if you were able to solve a problem, first by identifying what was wrong, then by taking the initiative to correct it. The military showed me that success

True mentors shine a light on talent.

> Success = determination, integrity, work ethic, and energy.

is not a fluke. To be recognized by your superiors, you have to take the initiative again and again.

In the context of the choice that Harper presented to me, I concluded that the correct path would complement the natural strengths he had recognized in me. If the company saw me as a fixer, then my interests were best served by taking the biggest risk possible.

Houston would not have been a big enough stretch. Geneva offered a foreign office with strong potential, but the language barrier was daunting and I felt it might prevent me from making a strong connection. A chance to prove myself at the parent company's New York headquarters was tempting, but again I felt the risk wasn't big enough. London would be the true test of leadership capabilities, the chance for growth and recognition.

London, I thought, needed the most fixing.

Monday morning I told Harper of my decision. He didn't seem surprised, probably having known all along which was the right fit. "I knew you'd understand you'd never become president of a company without first having run an office or gained international experience," Harper said.

I spent six years in London with my family, and though it was a time of dedicated, hard work, my wife and I look back on it with much fondness. Turning the UK office around was a challenge our team faced with great enthusiasm and energy. Once the business and leadership problems were addressed, I turned my focus to growth. Later, as president of McCann-Erickson Europe, I expanded its offices to fill out complete coverage of Europe. When I came back to New York in 1971 I was named president of the company and made a director of the Interpublic Group of Companies.

I stayed as president for two years, turning down a chance to take over Kentucky Fried Chicken, before leaving to become chairman of United Vintners, a division of Heublein. At the time it was the second largest wine company in the United States. I eventually became chairman and CEO of Heublein, now Diageo, before retiring in 1993.

Along the way I learned a great deal about myself and what it takes to be a success: determination, integrity, work ethic, talent, energy. Those are the obvious ones. What that weekend-long decision taught me was an unexpected concept—self-awareness. A fundamental characteristic of success is the ability to evaluate feedback from others and to use it to identify your strengths and capitalize on them.

Looking back, I believe Harper set me up to learn something about myself. He identified my talent and then allowed me the opportunity to cultivate it on my own. A true mentor will make it easier by shining a light on talent. The tricky part, though, is to understand yourself well enough to nurture what they see. I was proud to have learned of this critical part of my identity—my role in business—and I was determined to show Harper that he was right in what he saw.

MARTY RICHARDS

The best advice I can give to anyone who is young and has a dream is to always listen to your passion. The type of career doesn't matter. The big breaks are out there. Go with your heart and you will find them. Listen to the advice of others, but always hold their advice up to the light of your passion. You need tenacity and you need luck—but most of all, you need passion.

As a kid, I developed a passion for singing. I was always singing in my family's apartment and in the hallways of our building. Once, our next-door neighbor heard me singing as I stepped out of the elevator and remarked to my folks, "Your son can really sing. You ought to enroll him in some formal voice lessons."

They followed that suggestion, and by the age of eight, I was playing the newsboy in the Broadway production of *Mexican Hayride* with June Havoc and Bobby Clarke.

My folks grew concerned, though, for me and my passion for "the biz." Would I make enough money? Would I starve? Would I have a roof over my head when they were gone? At their insistence, I attended to my regular studies through high school, but I had already been hooked by my passion.

During and after high school, I worked professionally as a singer. I began winning contests on television, and later I graduated to playing the Copa, the Latin Quarter, the Living Room, Basin

MARTIN RICHARDS heads the film and theatrical production company The Producer Circle, which he founded with his late wife, Mary Lea Johnson, in 1976. Their first musical, *On the Twentieth Century*, won five Tony Awards. In his career, Richards's productions have won 38 Tony Awards, the Pulitzer Prize, seven Outer Critic Circle Awards and two New York Drama Critic Awards. His film production of *Chicago* won six Academy Awards, including his own as producer of the Best Picture of the Year. He lives in New York.

Street and Jack Silverman's International—all of which were some of the best rooms in New York. At Bon Soir, I opened for performers such as Herb Albert, Lainie Kazan, Lynn Carter and Barbra Streisand. I also sang solo on *The Ed Sullivan Show* and ended up recording for United Artists on the Ascot label and for Capitol Records.

My folks, however, remained apprehensive and urged me to further my education and go to college. They suggested I study architecture—I had displayed some interest in the subject at one time, and my grandfather and two uncles were successful architects and builders. All three were involved in the design team for Radio City Music Hall, among many other projects. I listened to my folks and enrolled at NYU as an architecture major—but I must confess, I didn't love it.

My passion remained singing.

Even though I appreciated my parents' intentions, I desperately missed singing. The first booking of my new manager, Shelley Schultz (he was Johnny Carson's manager at the time as well), was for me to play the lounge at the Sands Hotel in Las Vegas for the astronomical amount—or so it seemed to me—of $3,000 a week.

The problem, though, was that I was spending even more than that amount—roughly $4,000 a week—to pay for new arrangements, new acts, my own combo, my own rhythm section and my own travel expenses. At about that time, too, Elvis Presley was becoming popular and my kind of singing was going out of favor.

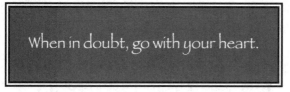

When in doubt, go with your heart.

I called Shelley and said, "I think I ought to quit."

"For God's sake, why?" he asked.

I explained my reasoning and told him that my mind was made up.

Since I had worked as a casting agent in between singing appearances, Tom Ward, who had been my first agent, asked if I wanted to work for him casting bit parts. I helped cast movies such as *On the Waterfront, Someone Up There Likes Me, Butterfield 8,* and *Funny Girl.* After three years, Tom offered me a partnership in his company, and I stayed there for an additional four years.

I went on to become the assistant to the head of casting, East Coast, for Twentieth Century Fox, where I began casting lead roles. While I was working there, I met Rue McClanahan. She asked me to come watch a scene from *Dylan* at The Actors Studio, so I did—and I thought she and the cast were incredibly

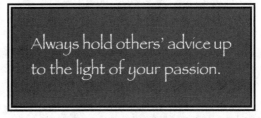

Always hold others' advice up to the light of your passion.

marvelous. In fact, the scene was so great that I asked if they would think about doing a revival of the show Off Broadway.

I had no idea how I was going to produce it. I wanted to do it, however, so I set about raising nearly $60,000 from family and friends. Eventually, I staged the production at the Mercer Arts Theatre with much success—Rue and the show won Obies and great acclaim. We were preparing to move the show to Broadway when the Theatre burned down, destroying all of our sets and costumes. Adding to our dismay, the investor who was going to give us the $250,000 to make the move decided instead to invest in the show that had been running across the street and had already posted its closing notice—a production called *Grease.*

That's show biz.

Right around then, theatrical producer Robert Fryer lost his longtime partner, Joe Harris, who decided it was time to get out of the business. Bobby and I had known each other since I cast *The Boston Strangler* with Tony Curtis for him. He asked if I would become involved with a new Broadway musical, *Chicago.* Gwen Verdon and Chita Rivera were the stars, and it was directed by Bob Fosse. I knew and admired all their work, so of course I said yes.

My first job was to raise $800,000, making *Chicago* the most expensive musical to be produced on Broadway at that time. I could not raise that amount from family and friends alone—I sang, acted and danced (sort of) the book and the score for I don't know how many people. The show opened on the road and received mixed reviews.

I was terrified. I was playing with so many people's money and with my own future as a producer, as well. So when the show opened on Broadway, I was incredibly apprehensive. To my great relief, though, we received extremely positive reviews.

Chicago became a major hit. It ran on Broadway for three years and was nominated for 11 Tony Awards. During that run I purchased the film rights to the show and began talking with Bob Fosse about directing the movie. Unfortunately, Bob passed away before we could make much progress.

It was not until much later that Harvey Weinstein called me about the project. Twenty-seven years after the opening of the original stage production; after forming my own production company, The Producer Circle; after 35 shows—one a Pulitzer Prize winner—and 38 Tony Awards, finally, I had the marvelous opportunity to produce *Chicago* as a motion picture. Rob Marshall agreed to direct the movie. The film won six Academy Awards, including my own as producer of the Best Picture of the Year.

My folks, as it turned out, never needed to worry about me starving. Sadly, my mom did not live long enough to enjoy my success, but my dad did. He was so proud of me and my fierce love for the profession. I also had the good fortune to share my life and my success with my dear wife, Mary Lea.

Always go with your heart. I love what I do today as much as I did when I was eight I still experience the same level of excitement when I get involved with any new project. Life is too short to not do what you love.

P.S. I'm still working.

JOHN M. RICHMAN

From my mid-teens on, I cannot remember a time when I wasn't working. Before going to college, I clerked and did inventory work in retail stores, sold magazines door to door and supervised younger children on school buses and in playground activities. I was undecided about my career path, although my stepfather was a career naval officer, so we moved quite often—and I knew I didn't want to do that.

I was fortunate to attend Yale University on scholarship, where I continued to work a variety of jobs—in kitchens, dining rooms, libraries and at the Yale Cooperative store. I spent the summers working at a record store in New York and serving as a desk clerk and tennis and swimming instructor at a resort hotel in Vermont.

None of those jobs, or my college education for that matter, really put me on a career path. My decision to attend law school, at Harvard, again on scholarship, was based more on the belief that law school would be intellectually stimulating and would provide good discipline and preparation than on a burning desire to practice law.

Upon graduation, however, I took a job at a small 15-man law firm in the Wall Street area. I found myself drawn to the corporate side of the company, specializing in the legal aspects of business

JOHN RICHMAN was chairman and chief executive officer of Kraft, Inc., from 1979 to 1989 after serving as Senior Vice President, Administration, and General Counsel of the company. Since 1990 he has been counsel for the law firm of Wachtell, Lipton, Rosen & Katz. He is active on many boards and charitable organizations in the Chicago area. Richman is a graduate of Yale University and earned his law degree at Harvard.

problems. Within a couple of years I made up my mind that what I wanted to do was work in a corporation's legal department.

By a stroke of good fortune, one of the companies looking for a young lawyer at that time was the National Dairy Products Corporation, whose corporate offices at the time were in New York. The company later moved its offices to suburban Chicago and changed its name to Kraft. I went to work there in 1954 and was fortunate enough to remain there in various capacities for 36 years.

I spent nine years in the legal department before becoming general counsel of a major division in 1963. That position provided me with my first opportunity to be a member of a management team. Seven years later, I became the senior vice president and general counsel of National Dairy.

The work was interesting and challenging, but I couldn't help the feeling that something was missing. A lawyer's role is really that of an advisor, not a decision maker, and that was what intrigued me about the corporate world. I wanted not just to give my opinion on the legal aspects of the situation, but to help solve the business problem at hand. Eventually people began asking me to do just that.

Still I was able to only give my opinion, and it was somebody else's job to make the actual decision—until Bill Beers took me under his wing, initially making me senior vice president, administration, with a wide variety of responsibilities, and then, in 1979, recommending to the board of directors that I succeed him as chairman and CEO of Kraft.

I really don't know what they saw in me to select me from other well qualified candidates, but obviously they thought I had done a good job at what I was asked to do and had been able to run a corporate division very well. It's kind of like picking a salesman to run a company—obviously you see something in him other than an ability to sell your product. I think most of my skeptics probably wondered how the company could pick a lawyer to run the company instead of somebody with more of a marketing background. I was determined to work hard to do the job, however, and I was fortunate to have somebody like Bill to teach me.

Bill and I were an odd combination. He was a self-styled cheese maker from rural Wisconsin, but the chemistry worked in our relationship. Bill helped me expand my horizons and capabilities, increasing my administrative responsibilities and putting me in charge of research projects that cut across division and departmental lines. Still, I was as surprised as everyone else when I was the choice to succeed Bill as chairman and CEO.

I spent 10 years in that position, as fascinating and challenging a position as anyone could hope to have. We were able to change the company from a sales-oriented organization to a more marketing-oriented one. We developed many outstanding executives who have gone on to run other corporations. We merged with Dart Industries and navigated the takeover of Kraft by Phillip Morris, which produced a great financial boon for Kraft shareholders.

My years in the business world have convinced me that someone cannot plan the breaks in his career—he or she can only plan to be prepared to take advantage of those breaks when they do occur. You can do that in a multitude of ways, but these seem to me to be the most important:

• Give 100 percent of your ability and integrity to everything you are called upon to do, even if the assignments seem boring or unimportant. Take pride in your work, both in terms of the results achieved and in terms of your own personal values.

• Treat everyone with the same respect, courtesy and candor that you expect from others.

• Act promptly and decisively. Gather all of the facts available to you, and make your decision based on the facts and the best information you have available at the time.

• Don't follow the all-too-common practice of denigrating your competitors, but try to understand their situations and anticipate their actions. Never prepare an action plan without asking yourself what the competitive response will be.

• Finally, be flexible and open to new ideas and new opportunities. You can never tell where that break is going to come from.

JOHN ROACH

Do your job the best it can be done. That's certainly what worked for me.

In 1968, I was working for the Tandy Corporation as the head of data processing (now referred to as information services), and I was part of a group of accounting executives who developed a system to computerize our profit and loss statements.

The biggest problem we had with the project was that we had to report to our boss, Charles Tandy, about it. Mr. Tandy was not a particular fan of computer systems at that time. As the newest member of management, I was selected by my peers to make the presentation. I wouldn't say I was scared, but I did wonder what his reaction was going to be because he considered the profit and loss statements to be "the Bible."

I prepared well for the meeting. I had a list of benefits that the computer system would have over the manual system. We were beginning to grow the RadioShack chain rapidly, so one of the benefits was that we would be able to generate the profit and loss statements three days earlier.

You never really got in trouble with Charles Tandy, but he could give you significant ridicule to make you wonder if you were smart enough to know what you were doing. He was an entrepreneur, a financier, a retailer and an incredible teacher. He spent a lot

JOHN V. ROACH is chairman of the board emeritus of the former Tandy Corporation, which was renamed RadioShack Corporation in 2000. He served as the chairman of the board and CEO of Tandy Corp. from 1982 to 1999. Roach joined Tandy Computer Services in 1967 and served in a variety of positions before becoming president and chief operating officer in 1980. He also serves as the chairman of the board of Texas Christian University.

of time teaching as he talked about business issues, and he didn't mince any words. He often used negative motivation.

Charles listened to what I had to say, then took a puff of his big cigar and said, "The store in Bakersfield, California has been losing money for three months. If you had gotten the P&Ls three days sooner, I would have known for two months and twenty-seven days the store was losing money. It doesn't make a damn bit of difference when you get the P&Ls out—it's what you do with the information when you get it."

He was right, and it was a strong message.

Charles was always big on performance, and he gave his managers a lot of authority to make the right decisions—but he always held people accountable for those decisions. He believed in the company and almost forced employees to borrow money to buy stock. He was disappointed when one didn't do it. Charles used the idea of profit-based bonuses as a way to motivate his employees.

My responsibilities included helping to bring some order to the reporting of our various companies and to encourage management to utilize our entrepreneurial philosophies. In 1970, when I spent a day in discussion with Tandy about my bonus for the year, he concluded that I had not been as effective as I could have been, and he therefore was not going to increase my bonus. Increases in base pay were rarely given. In the following days, several other executives tried to lobby Tandy on my behalf but to no avail.

Over the next year I voluntarily took on the task of cleaning up the accounts receivable of a new acquisition, Allied Electronics. I spent about 20 weeks away from Fort Worth, working on it in Chicago. When bonus time came around again, after a full day of discussion, Tandy told me to "just write down whatever bonus you want." It wasn't easy, but I wrote down a number that was about 170 percent of my base pay. Tandy agreed, but the check wasn't forthcoming.

When I finally inquired about it later, he pulled the check out of his pocket and said he would give it to me when the Allied receivables reached a certain level. I called my bank and told them I couldn't pay my loan for stock purchases or living expenses until

I got that check. Periodically, I would hear that Tandy pulled that by-then-tattered check out of his pocket as a way of triumphantly telling other executives that he demanded results before employees would be rewarded.

This went on for about two months, before I decided to ask Tandy to call my bank himself and explain my predicament. Later that day, with strong encouragement from a senior officer, Tandy gave me the check, "even though you haven't earned it."

He died in 1978, at the age of 60, and a couple of years later I was named chairman and chief executive officer. I tried to adapt and embrace to a large extent his philosophies but not his demeanor. The key to our company's growth was that we had employees who were empowered and performed their jobs very well. Using that entrepreneurial culture we were able to take risks with products that worked.

We put together a small team that introduced the first micro-computer system to be sold at retail nationwide—the TRS-80. We developed this system for $150,000 because no traditional computer company thought it was a viable product. They certainly changed their mind after they saw our success.

We drove a hard bargain with Bill Gates and the fledgling Microsoft Company that gave them early credibility. We developed a venture with Nokia that introduced them to low-cost manufacturing of cellular phones and to the U.S. market. We provided major distribution to AOL that helped them finance early growth. Those were only some of our successes.

What young employees and executives need to understand is that, if they are continuously performing at a high level at whatever job they have, they are going to give themselves a greater chance at recognition when a greater opportunity comes along.

I have heard a lot of Monday morning quarterbacks say, "If I were the boss, we would do this or that." What those people need to realize is that if they do their current job exceptionally well in the present, they might just get that chance to run their company in the future.

WILBUR ROSS

In 1958, during March of my junior year at Yale, I received the phone call that would change my life.

Horace Islieb, the university treasurer and faculty adviser to my fraternity, was calling to find out what my plans were for the summer. I told Mr. Islieb that I was most likely going back to my old job, parking cars at Monmouth Park Jockey Club.

"No, you need a job that can lead to something," he said. "I'm leaving the university to become a partner in a boutique money management firm, Buckner & Co., and you can be a summer trainee there."

He arranged for me to start the day after my last class, and that summer convinced me what I wanted to do when I completed school. Working for Buckner & Co. was a wonderful experience.

Pete Buckner was the son-in-law of IBM's Tom Watson, and he was also the board chairman of the Salvation Army. The firm managed portfolios for wealthy families and their foundations. The partners were experienced deep value equity investors who bought out-of-favor, distressed stocks and also specialized in high yielding, low quality tax-exempt bonds.

At eight o'clock every morning we met in Mr. Buckner's office, he read a passage from the Bible, and we spent five minutes

WILBUR ROSS may be the best known turnaround financier in the United States, having been involved in the restructuring of more than $200 billion of defaulted companies' assets around the world. Ross organized International Steel Group in 2002 and through its acquisitions it is now the largest integrated steel company in North America. Ross is a graduate of Yale University and earned an MBA, with distinction, at Harvard University.

in meditation. Then we made our game plan for the day's trading. At first, I had no idea what everyone was talking about, but I paid attention and stayed up late at night studying books on securities analysis. By the end of the summer, I felt brave enough to recommend a bond or two.

After returning to school, I received a letter from J.P. Morgan and Co. Mr. Islieb had struck again. He had arranged for me to go to New York to be interviewed for a

> Study why companies fail—you'll learn more than why companies succeed.

job in the J.P. Morgan training program. Eventually two classmates and I were hired, and after a week working in the mailroom, we moved on to other, more sophisticated departments.

One day late that summer, I was sent to a closing in the offices of William Zeckendorf Sr., the legendary real estate speculator. A Morgan client had lent Zeckendorf money and after a restructuring, was to receive a 13th mortgage on a Fifth Avenue office building. I couldn't get my mind off the fact that a 13th mortgage was an asset, but it was my first closing on behalf of the bank, so I was nervous and got there a half-hour early.

The receptionist ushered me into an empty office, which provided a magnificent wraparound view of the entire city. I was standing there when a great bear of a man carrying a tiny Chihuahua walked up and put his hand on my shoulder.

"What's the matter, son?" he asked.

"Nothing, sir," I said. "It's just that I've never seen a completely circular office."

He bent down closer to me and said in a raspy whisper, "Let me tell you something. If you had been backed into a corner as many times as I have, you would have a god-damned round office too."

The lessons I learned from both of my summer jobs stayed with me as I graduated and entered Harvard Business School, where I came under the guidance of another of Mr. Islieb's friends, General Georges Doriot, a French national who had immigrated to the United States just before World War II and had become a general in the Quartermaster Corps.

He later founded American Research and Development Corp., one of the earliest venture capital firms, which became very successful. He taught a class called "Manufacturing" that really was about his insights into business. He regularly brought in famous businessmen as guest speakers.

One of the lessons he stressed was that you often learn more by studying why some companies fail than you do by studying what made others succeed. He taught me that business was a lot like playing tennis—the key to success often is remaining steady and patient and waiting to take advantage of your opponent's mistakes. If you keep hitting the ball deep and run your opponent back and forth, he will eventually hit a short shot that you can put away. Don't try to put away every shot, but wait for the opening and the shot you can hit for a winner.

Most of the mistakes people make in business come from ill-timed, rash behavior. Business decisions often tend to be very emotional, and to be successful you have to be able to keep your emotions separate from the decision-making process. The rule of thumb I have always tried to follow is that if something gets me upset, I try not to react to it on the spot. I sleep on it, and then make my decision when I am calm.

I also encourage young professionals to find a particular area of business they enjoy and become an expert at it. People who can develop specialized skills have a great chance to be successful.

The lessons that Horace Islieb and General Doriot taught me years ago have stayed with me as I moved through the business world. As head of the International Steel Group, I still use their advice every day. Even now, after $200 billion of corporate restructurings, I am constantly amazed at how correct their insights were and how applicable they are to today's business environment.

> Separate emotion from solid analysis—rash behavior leads to poor decisions.

WILLIAM J. RUANE

Believe it or not, my big break in business came from reading a book!

As I was preparing to leave the navy after World War II, I really had no idea what career I was going to pursue. I had obtained an engineering degree in the navy, but was not convinced I wanted to do that for the rest of my life.

I met with a guidance officer, who suggested I apply for the Harvard Business School. I had thought about trying to get some supplemental education and had heard of Harvard, but I had never heard of the Harvard Business School. My naiveté showed when I decided to fill out an application and went there to submit it to the admissions office in August of 1946. The people in the office looked at me and said, "Are you serious? School starts next week. You don't have a prayer of being admitted."

The folks there were nice enough to see me, however, and said they would put the application in their files, but with no guarantee that I would be accepted in the future. I left and got a job working as a test engineer for General Electric. A year later I reapplied and was accepted at the school.

One of the classes at Harvard was Investment Management, taught by Professor George Bates. During the two-year program, this was the only class I took that required the students to read a

WILLIAM RUANE joined Kidder, Peabody & Co. in 1949 and remained there until he founded Ruane Cunniff in 1969. At Kidder Peabody he became a vice president, a member of the investment committee and a manager of the Special Investment Advisory Service. A graduate of the University of Minnesota, Ruane earned his MBA at the Harvard Business School.

book. All of the other classes were designed to study particular business cases. The book Professor Bates required his students to read was called *Security Analysis* by Ben Graham. I was immediately hooked—Graham was a genius!

The book detailed Graham's logic of how to evaluate a company and determine its worth, which let you decide if it was a good stock 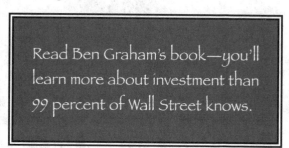 to buy. The book described the futility of trying to select attractive stocks by the historical price movements, known as technical analysis, and by hunch and intuition. It simply explained that the current price of a company's stock, times the number of shares outstanding, plus any debt equals the value of the company on any particular day.

For the sake of an example, say that number turns out to be $500 million on a particular day. A critical study based on the principles of security analysis, however, finds that the intrinsic value of the company is actually about $1 billion. This discrepancy would lead me to buy the stock with a margin of safety and a strong expectation of an attractive return in time.

Graham's theory was that in the short term, the stock market is like an election, where anybody can vote, but over the long term, the market is more like a scale, which weighs the values properly.

My interest in Graham's philosophies prompted me to ask if I could attend a seminar he was conducting at Columbia University in 1951, even though I was not a student there. Reading this book, and studying under Graham, significantly changed my life.

One of the students I met in the seminar was Warren Buffett, whose admiration of Graham led him to be Graham's major disciple. The opportunity to develop a friendship with Mr. Buffett ranks right along with my top personal and business breaks.

Upon graduation in 1949, my interest in investments took me to Wall Street. It was not a popular place at that time—only eight members of our class of 645 did the same. I went to work at Kidder Peabody and remained there for 20 years before forming my own firm using the principles of security analysis in our investment management firm.

Every chief financial officer of every corporation in America should read *Security Analysis*. If they had read the book and put its principles into action, the corporate world would never have had the scandals that it's experienced in recent years. It details an outline of business principles that every CFO should follow if they want to provide ethical and honest reports.

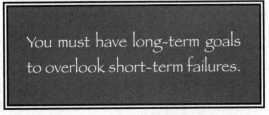

You must have long-term goals to overlook short-term failures.

Over the years a lot of young people have come to me and said they were thinking about going into the business world. My advice to them has been to read Graham's book. I said if you read this book and enjoy it, you will know more about investments and the value of stocks than 95 percent of the people on Wall Street.

MURIEL SIEBERT

When I left my home in Cleveland in 1954 for a new life in New York, I really had no idea how I was going to earn a living. I had dropped out of college when my father became ill and eventually died from cancer at the age of 52, and here I was driving down the road in a used Studebaker and with $500 in my pocket.

My sister was living in New York, so I knew I would have a bed while I looked for a job. I had been away from my home and family only once before, on a trip to New York the previous year. I think the real reason why I decided not to return to college and instead head for New York was, "Why not? Let's see what the world is like."

On that first trip to New York, I had taken a tour of the New York Stock Exchange. It looked exciting, but I really didn't have my mind set on working there. I did know that if I had a talent, it was an ability to look at a page of numbers and make them light up and tell a story. When I took accounting courses in college, I could come in and pass the tests without even going to class.

Do not, however, ask me to spell.

I applied for a job at the United Nations because my cousin was one of the representatives there, but I didn't get it because I didn't speak two languages. I then applied for a job with Merrill

MURIEL "MICKIE" SIEBERT is the founder and president of the New York Stock Exchange brokerage firm that bears her name, Muriel Siebert & Co., Inc. She established the firm in 1967 when she became the first woman member of the NYSE. She took a leave of absence from her firm in 1977 to serve as the first woman Superintendent of Banking for the state of New York. She also is actively involved in a wide range of non-profit, civic and women's organizations. Her autobiography, *Changing the Rules: Adventures of a Wall Street Maverick* was published by Simon and Schuster in 2002.

Lynch, and they asked if I had a college degree. When I said no, they said no job. I went down the street and applied for a job at Bache and Co. I told them I was pretty good with numbers, and they kept asking me questions, almost like a test. When it was over they said I could take a job in the accounting department for $75 a week or a job as a trainee in the research department for $65 a week. I took the job in research.

One of the senior analysts gave me two industries as my area of responsibility, the airline industry and radio, television and motion pictures. This, in reality, might have turned out to be my big break because, in the 1950s, both of these industries were just beginning to blossom.

One of the first realizations I came to was that the old motion pictures were totally depreciated on the books and had to have substantial value for television. I was the first analyst covering that industry who saw the value that those films had for television, and I wrote a recommendation of the industry. It proved that I was correct.

Having that recommendation in my portfolio helped me build a reputation pretty fast. I doubled my salary in two and a half years to $130 a week, but when I found out men who had the same job I did were making $200 to $225 a week, it was time for me to go somewhere else. That difference is a quality of life difference.

My career continued to develop as more of my recommendations proved to be correct. The biggest obstacle I faced, however, was a pervasive discrimination against my gender. Men in this industry at that time were reluctant to accept the suggestions and recommendations of a woman, and most of the major firms were not willing to hire a woman and pay her at the same rate they would a man in the same position.

For that reason I continued to work for smaller firms, as a partner, and I learned a great deal about the business. I helped Lockheed when it was in trouble. I worked with its lobbyists and met with many senators. Working for a six- or eight-person firm, even though I was a partner, was very limiting.

Because I knew no major firm would hire or pay me equally, I decided to take the gamble of opening my own firm—and applied to become the first woman member of the New York Stock Exchange. This was in 1967. Nine of the first 10 men I asked to sponsor my application turned me down.

Before considering me for membership, the Stock Exchange said I had to have a letter from a bank agreeing to lend me $300,000 of the $445,000 it cost to buy a seat on the Exchange. At that time I was in a Catch 22 situation: I couldn't get the seat without securing the loan, and I was having trouble securing the loan without first getting the seat. Ultimately, J.P. Morgan agreed to make the loan.

Being able to buy that seat on the Exchange changed my life, and it changed that industry for all women. In the past, women had applied but the Exchange had refused their applications. People trusted me, and luckily I was able to repay that trust. At that time our word was our bond, and we would sooner go broke before we would break our word.

The industry has changed over time to present many more opportunities for women. Even those who are not in the investment business take a greater interest in financial matters today and are much more conscious of how to save and invest money.

One of the biggest differences since the early days of my career is that men are now willing to take advice from women, and they have no qualms about working with a woman. People usually end up realizing that, whether it is a man or woman doing the job, it is very easy to track their performance. What matters are the results, and that's the way it should be.

My success was built on working hard and proving that I could succeed in a man's world. I don't consider that I was trying to break down any walls or to be any kind of rebel. I just wanted to have the same opportunities a man had. If I could do the same job as well or better, my opinion was that the fact I was a woman should make no difference.

All I tried to do was treat everybody the way I liked to be treated. I tried to always use common sense, and one value I never compromised was my integrity. If you do that you have a great chance to be successful, whether you are a man or a woman, no matter the industry.

JOHN G. SMALE

In the fall of 1952, I really needed a job.

I had graduated from Miami (Ohio) University in 1949 and had worked briefly for two companies, the second of which was a start-up operation making an over-the-counter nose drop.

That company was quickly running out of money. When my wife gave birth to our first child, I signed over my paycheck to my father-in-law to cover the hospital expenses—and the check bounced.

To say I was getting desperate when I saw the Procter & Gamble ad in the *Chicago Tribune* is definitely an understatement.

So I answered the ad, and after an on-site interview in Cincinnati on a Friday, I received a phone call on the following Monday asking if I could start work within a couple of weeks. I said, "I will be there on Wednesday."

I really needed to be on somebody's payroll.

Joining Procter & Gamble was the first big break of my career. From the moment I walked in the door I was challenged, mentored, encouraged and pretty much delighted with what I was doing at any given point in time.

I had been working in brand management on the Gleem account for six years when I was promoted to associate advertising manager on the Crest toothpaste account. Crest had been intro-

JOHN SMALE became president of Procter & Gamble in 1974 and was named chief executive officer in 1981. He added the chairman of the board to his duties in 1986 and served in those capacities until his retirement in 1990, which ended his 38-year career with the company. A graduate of Miami (Ohio) University, Smale remains active in many civic and charitable organizations. He and his wife, Phyllis, are the parents of four children.

duced by Procter & Gamble in 1955 after it was developed by
P&G scientists working with Indiana University. It was the first
clinically proven effective anti-decay toothpaste.

There was a great deal of competition in the industry at the
time, and we were having trouble breaking out. There were a number of products that said they could prevent tooth decay, and we
needed something that would separate Crest from the rest.

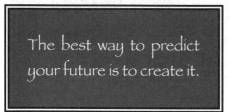

The best way to predict
your future is to create it.

What gave us that
edge was an advertising
campaign created by our ad
agency, Benton & Bowles,
that featured the slogan,
"Look,   Mom,   No
Cavities." This campaign was launched in 1958, when Crest had
only a seven to eight percent share of the market. Over the next
two years our share of the market increased to 12 to 13 percent.

At about the same time, we had begun working with the
American Dental Association, seeking their endorsement that
Crest really did prevent tooth decay. We went through more clin-
ical tests, and finally in August 1960, the American Dental
Association endorsed Crest.

That endorsement was national news, and the brand took off
dramatically. Shipments to retailers had to be back-ordered for several months as we rushed to increase our production capacity.
Within three years, Crest's share of the market had risen to 30 percent and we were firmly established as the market leader.

Those five years were among the most exciting of my career.
I welcomed the challenge, as does any brand manager, of trying to
hold and grow our share of the market. You are always fighting to
improve your product and its acceptance and to find the best way
to express that. You have to persuade the customer that you have
the best product.

As I continued to move up the corporate ladder at Procter &
Gamble, the nature of the challenges changed. We faced the
dilemma of what to do with our Rely tampons when the toxic
shock syndrome crisis developed in the 1970s. Even though we

thought our product was targeted unfairly, we pulled the product off the market.

Luckily we were a strong enough and diverse enough company that our other business lines were able to carry us when one of the product lines was struggling. We also grew internationally to the point where more than half of the company's business now comes from outside the United States.

The key to my enjoyment at Procter & Gamble was that the challenges were always exciting. I always try to tell young people that when they are looking for a career they need to look for something they really enjoy doing. If you don't have a passion for what you are doing, you need to keep looking. If you take pleasure in what you are doing, it truly isn't work, and the future will take care of itself.

That's another mistake too many young people make—they are overly worried about the future and try to plan where they will be at some later point in their careers. They keep worrying about gaining more and more responsibility and authority, instead of just trying to do a good job at what they are doing. If you do that, the responsibility and authority will just come naturally.

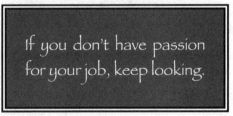
If you don't have passion for your job, keep looking.

My own reward was seeing the brand that I was working on flourishing. I was fortunate to work for a company that was governed very much by principle. The people who ran the company were totally focused on rewarding its employees on the basis of merit. They appreciated jobs well done and treated everyone that way. That was a tremendous incentive for young people to see that and to be on the receiving end of those rewards.

JOEL SMILOW

I was working for a marketing consulting firm in Connecticut in 1969 when an executive search firm contacted me about an opening for a vice president of marketing for International Latex Inc., now known as Playtex. Though I really wasn't interested in the job, the company or commuting to New York, I went to the interview with the company's president, Bernhardt Denmark, because I always enjoyed meeting senior business executives and because I thought there was a chance I might be able to get the company to become a client of my company.

The interview went well, and I was very impressed with Bernie, both personally and professionally. I declined the position, but we met several times over the next few months as he tried to talk me into taking another job as the vice president international. I turned that job down too, but I was successful in getting the company to hire our firm's European division as a consultant for its operations in Germany.

In September, Bernie called and asked me to meet him on Sunday at his suburban, weekend home. I had no idea why he wanted to meet and he didn't give me any hint until I arrived at his house. He greeted me basically by saying, "As you may or may not know [I didn't], we have been looking for my replacement as president of International Latex for the last two or three months."

JOEL E. SMILOW began his business career in the marketing department of Procter & Gamble before joining Glendinning Associates, a marketing consulting firm. He was hired as president of the International Latex Corp. (Playtex) in 1969. In 1975 his company was acquired by Esmark Inc. and Smilow became chairman and CEO of a sub-holding company composed of Playtex, Max Factor, Almay, McCall Pattern and Halston. In 1984 Esmark was acquired by Beatrice Companies and Smilow was placed in charge of its non-food companies. In 1986 he led a leveraged buyout of Playtex and became the CEO of Playtex. Smilow retired in 1995 but remains active with investment and philanthropic activities.

Bernie had been promoted to president of the parent company, Glen Alden.

Bernie went on to say that he had interviewed at least a dozen candidates for the job, all of whom were at least 15 years older than me—I was 36 at the time—and all of whom had had much broader experiences and responsibilities. Many had already been presidents of corporations or divisions. He added, however, that he felt I "could do more for the company than any of the others and therefore you are a candidate—what do you think of that?"

Frankly, I liked it a lot. We talked for a couple of hours. Subsequently, we met twice more before he formally offered me the job of president of International Latex and I accepted the job.

As we walked back to his New York apartment after the job-offer dinner, he said, "This just has to work." I agreed, but questioned why he had said it in those terms. Bernie added, "Because if you fail, people will think I am crazy to have hired someone so young, with no real experience in any area other than marketing and no international experience to run a global company with thousands of employees."

I felt I was ready for the challenge. I knew I had to prove I could be a strong leader for the company, but I didn't feel insecure or have any doubts that I could do the job.

Even though I did not have the experience of many

> My motto for success as a leader is: "As above, so below."

of the other candidates, I had learned a great deal in my business life. I had graduated from Yale, served for two years in the navy, received my MBA from Harvard Business School and spent almost seven years in marketing at Procter & Gamble before joining the marketing consulting firm in 1965.

I knew I still had a lot to learn, though, and I believe one of the reasons everything worked out so well was that I asked a lot of questions and tried to get as much input as I could from all areas of the company.

Playtex, which was founded in the 1930s, has always had the same motto. It is four simple words, which I've always believed in and tried to practice: As above, so below.

One of the best things I did was spend my first month with the company working in the field as a member of the sales force. I did all of the jobs, going up and down the streets, counting stock, rearranging the product on the shelves, everything. I knew the sales department was really the heart and soul of the company, and spending that time working with them really helped my understanding of the culture and furthered my acceptance by the employees.

Bernie left International Latex about nine months after I started. The company performed very well through five changes of control, the last of which was a billion-dollar leveraged buyout of the company that I led in December 1986, 17 years after I was named president.

> The sales department is the heart of most companies—working there teaches you the company culture.

Bernie and his wife, Muriel, remain great friends of mine, some 35 years after we first met. I never have ceased to be in awe of the self-confidence, vision and judgment that enabled him to make the key hiring decision that resulted in "my biggest break."

DENNIS SMITH

When I began keeping notes on my everyday experiences as a firefighter in the South Bronx, there was no way of predicting that it would one day become a book that would be translated into 12 languages, go through seven printings and sell more than two million copies.

I had been asked to write an article for *True* magazine about the life of a modern-day firefighter, based on a letter of literary criticism I had written to the *New York Times Book Review*. I had never met a person in the publishing industry.

I worked in the South Bronx at Engine Company 82 from 1966 to 1973 and it was then the busiest fire company in the most desperate neighborhood in New York. Records were set there for crime, poverty, illness and other deprivation. Our company responded to about 9,000 alarms a year, about one-third for emergencies such as car accidents, shootings and drug overdoses. Another third were false alarms. The final third were for fires.

In our district, an average day included about 10 or 12 calls to fires, many of which were deliberately set. Many also were serious, presenting a great degree of danger to those called on to try to put out the fire.

The experience really was similar to those engaged in war, with each day offering a different set of challenges. The assignment

DENNIS SMITH is a former firefighter and is the best-known, most trusted leader and adviser to firefighters in the United States. Smith spent 18 years as a firefighter in New York, and used his experiences to write *Report From Engine Co. 82*, which became a bestseller and launched his writing career. He is the author of 12 books, founded a national magazine for firefighters and created an affinity financial services company directed to firefighters. For the past 18 years he also has been the president or chairman of Kips Bay Boys and Girls Club in the Bronx where 9,000 youngsters are members.

to write about these brave men was almost as frightening as the first time I pushed a hose line into a burning building.

Finding the time to write was one of the challenges. Between working 40 hours a week, being a husband and a father of three kids, going to classes at New York University for my master's degree and working a second job as a limo driver to try to pay the bills did not leave a lot of free time.

Not long after my letter appeared in the *Times*, I was featured in a story in *The New Yorker* magazine. An editor for McCall Books saw the story and asked if I had ever

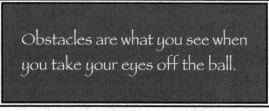

Obstacles are what you see when you take your eyes off the ball.

considered writing a book about my life as a firefighter.

The result was *Report from Engine Co. 82*, the book that changed my life.

Since its publication I have gone on to write eleven other books, create a national magazine for firefighters, *Firehouse*, start several businesses relating to firefighting, and form the Foundation for the Health and Safety of American Firefighters. I couldn't have done any of those things without having written and published that book.

The book gave me a platform to address the critical issues facing firefighters at that time, and which continue to face firefighters and all first responders today. It is a privilege for me to represent such courageous, committed people.

A common misconception is that the only thing firefighters do is fight fires. That could not be further from the truth. Think of any natural disaster you have witnessed on television. Think of the terrorist attacks of September 11, think of car accidents and other incidents of violence. In all of those cases, firefighters, paid or volunteer, were there, often facing great personal danger, trying to help and comfort the victims.

In any major city in this country, the sirens of fire engines often fill the air. Everybody gets out of their way, but they don't stop to think about how difficult the firefighter's job is or the

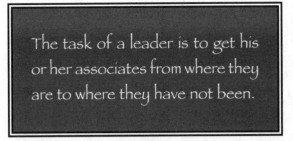

The task of a leader is to get his or her associates from where they are to where they have not been.

numerous variables that must be considered. What is the construction of the building on fire? How is the fire traveling? Are people trapped in the building? Are there victims of other crimes such as a shooting involved? Did any of the people involved suffer a heart attack or seizure? A firefighter has to be prepared to deal with all those challenges and more.

These questions, and the firefighter's answers, often determine life and death.

Firefighters are human beings, like you or your neighbor. Yet they are different. What separates them is their dedication to their job, to the challenge they face and accept on a daily basis. When that alarm rings in the firehouse, they always answer it.

JERRE L. STEAD

When I was hired by Honeywell in 1965, having just graduated from the University of Iowa, I was assigned to a one-year training program, during the course of which I was supposed to work in many different departments. That assignment began on June 14, and less than a month later, on July 5, I was called in and told that my year of training was up. I was going to be the new foreman at the assembly plant in Minneapolis.

Just a couple of months out of school, and all of a sudden I was in charge of 400 people and three shifts. I sensed it would be a great challenge, particularly because I would be supervising workers who were much older than me. The previous foreman decided it was simply too much work and left.

It was a challenge that I looked forward to, because I knew I would enjoy the job and wondered what I had been missing. As it turned out, I was able to communicate well the employees, especially considering the age difference. I strove to gain their respect, and when I was able to do that it made everyone more comfortable and the whole work environment more enjoyable.

It was a very fine line that I had to walk—I could understand where there would be resentment and jealousy—but it also was a great learning experience. I was able to earn the workers' respect simply by performing well.

JERRE STEAD became executive chairman of HIS/HAIC in 2001 after retiring as chairman and CEO of Ingram Micro in 2000. Under his leadership Ingram Micro went public with the largest IPO in history for a technology company in 1996. The company grew from $8 million to more than $30 million and is now doing business in 120 countries. Stead spent 21 years at Honeywell, Inc., and held a number of executive management positions in the United States and Europe. He also served as CEO of Square D Co. and AT&T's Global Business Communications Systems. A graduate of the University of Iowa, Stead has served on 27 corporate boards during his career.

I moved through a variety of jobs at Honeywell. I had 18 different leaders in my 21 years there, and I really learned a lot about what worked and what didn't work and the reasons behind those results. It really came down to a fundamental belief that if you are going to be successful you have to help others be successful. Nobody can do it by themselves.

I had never thought about leaving Honeywell until 1985. That year, the company was celebrating its 100th anniversary, and I was asked to chair a small top executive committee to help evaluate and make recommendations about the company's future. I had been working for Honeywell for 20 years and had reached the level of group vice president.

One of the companies that we investigated was Square D, a leading manufacturer of electrical distribution and factory automation products. Our committee ultimately recommended that Honeywell make an offer to buy the company.

The Honeywell board approved the plan, but when we made the offer Square D told us they were not interested in selling the company. We forgot about it and moved on to the next company on our list.

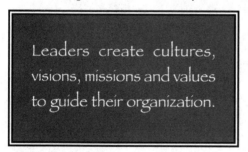

Leaders create cultures, visions, missions and values to guide their organization.

A short time later, I received a phone call from Square D wondering if I would be interested in becoming the president and chief operating officer of their company. I turned down the offer, just as the company had rejected Honeywell's purchase offer.

The company was persistent, however, and kept calling to see if I would change my mind. I knew the company well because of all the research Honeywell's committee had done. I thought it was a company with enormous potential because it had great products and great people, but was not being as aggressive in the marketplace as I thought it could be. Finally, in December 1986, after almost six months of talking with Square D, I said yes to their offer.

Getting that offer from Square D turned out to be the biggest break of my career.

I was able to help the company change its way of doing business, going from a philosophy of focusing on what they were doing in the present to one of always looking ahead to find the next big jump the company could take.

We became more aggressive, especially overseas. It was an area the company had not taken advantage of. Our sales growth was excellent, and five years later when the company was sold, the shareholders received an excellent return for their investment.

Since that time I have been fortunate to serve as chairman and CEO of four other outstanding companies. One of the things I am most proud of is that 29 people who worked with or for me over the years have gone on to serve as CEOs of other corporations.

I hope they have learned a lot of the same lessons I learned over the years. So many keys to business success seem so logical, yet so many people don't ever seem to understand how important they are.

I learned at a young age how important it is to take personal responsibility and to treat all people with equal dignity and respect. You have to be more focused on the success of the company as a whole rather than solely on individual success. Leaders of companies have to create the culture, vision, mission and values that lead to the processes by which great people do great things.

In my opinion, it is important for young professionals to get international experience as soon as they can. You have to learn to listen—don't waste time or energy on things that people do not feel good about. It is a simple philosophy, but it works.

Perhaps most importantly, you have to stay in the best physical and mental shape possible. I have always been amazed at the number of people who have great talent but get burned out, and I think a big part of that is their physical condition. It's going to be even more important in the future, because the world is only going to move even faster. What you are really doing in business is running a marathon that never ends.

DANIEL P. TULLY

When I was growing up, everyone in my family was a steam fitter, which was a blue-collar, union job. So my parents were shocked when I said I wanted to attend college instead of continuing that tradition.

After graduating from St. John's University with a degree in accounting, and then service in the army, I was ready for my first "real" job. I went to St. John's job placement center and found out three firms were hiring—U.S. Steel, Durkee Foods, and Merrill Lynch, Pierce, Fenner & Beane.

When I called Merrill, they agreed to see me that afternoon. I was hired on the spot and started the next day as a junior accountant. I didn't know what the company did, and neither did anybody in my family. When I told my mother about the job, she replied, "Good, I always thought you'd do well in advertising."

Getting hired by a firm like Merrill Lynch was truly my big break. I never left the company, ultimately rising to the position of chairman and CEO. The way Charles Merrill and Winthrop Smith built the firm on ethical principles impacted my entire life and career. The principles complemented the way I had been raised and what my parents had taught me about fair dealing and the right way to treat people. Together those lessons created a mosaic that helped guide me throughout my life.

DANIEL P. TULLY is chairman emeritus of Merrill Lynch & Co., Inc., the worldwide financial services corporation. He spent his entire business career at Merrill Lynch, joining the firm in the accounting department in 1955. He rose through the company's ranks, working in a variety of positions, before becoming CEO in 1992 and chairman of the board in 1993. Tully orchestrated the company's shift from a product-driven sales effort to a client-focused marketing approach. He is a graduate of St. John's University and completed Harvard Business School's Advanced Management Program. He and his wife, Grace, have four children and 14 grandchildren and reside in Darien, Connecticut.

It turned out I wasn't smart enough to be a great accountant, but I got an opportunity to work on the client side. It was a good fit for me. I was able to combine the business skills I learned in my CPA training and my understanding of finance with the ability to build relationships and the compassion for all human beings that I had learned growing up in Queens. Doing right by clients and colleagues is really an extension of doing right by friends, neighbors and family.

Early in my career, I was assigned to the company's office in Stamford, Connecticut. I was given the chance to participate in many local charities, which enabled me to meet very successful, affluent people. I learned from them and built a successful business. It was in the Stamford office, during a national crisis, that I was first recognized as a potential leader.

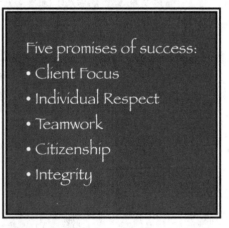

I was in the office on November 22, 1963, when president John F. Kennedy was assassinated in Dallas. It was about 1:00 p.m. on Friday, and the phones began to ring off the hook. People felt the world was ending. Clients and employees alike were panicked and looked to me for constant, steady reassurance.

Five promises of success:
- Client Focus
- Individual Respect
- Teamwork
- Citizenship
- Integrity

My work that day, in the days that followed and when the markets reopened caught the attention of my superiors. Being able to stay calm in a crisis was a challenge I would face several times later in my career—during the Hunt Silver crisis, the Mortgage Backed Crisis in 1987, the Crash of October 19, 1987, and the Orange County bankruptcy of 1993, just to name a few.

The quality of being easily alarmed has no place in management and certainly not in dealing with people's assets. There's never a reason to panic; ultimately principles and values will win.

I moved from Stamford to the firm's headquarters in New York to become marketing director—a giant promotion—and then kept moving up the corporate ladder. I had intended to retire at the age of 55, but when I became the chief operating officer and realized there was a chance I could become chairman and CEO, I decided to stick around.

One reason I think I was able to move up through the company was that I was never looking or campaigning for the next job. I trusted my bosses and thought that, if I worked hard and did my job well, my performance would be noticed. I think that's the way it is in most companies.

Merrill Lynch made certain that our clients were our first priority. The company fostered an environment where people felt included and considered themselves to be part of something great. Don Regan, one of my predecessors, treated everyone with respect and dignity. When the guy who shined shoes walked through the office, Don would talk with him about his family and his plans for the weekend. The next person Don spoke with might be the president of the United States. Everyone received the same personal focus and 100 percent of Don's attention.

The idea of treating everyone well, of making everyone feel included and using that as a basis of a culture to provide outstanding client service, is really at the heart of the Merrill Lynch set of principles. When I assumed responsibility for leading the firm, the first thing I did was to launch a program to rearticulate the principles. I wanted to make certain all employees understood them and made them a part of their everyday lives.

Not many people at that time remembered Charles Merrill and Winthrop Smith or the way Merrill Lynch was built. When we placed the principles in granite in the lobby, they knew we were serious about reinvigorating a culture centered on those principles. I knew we had succeeded when our investment bankers started putting the principles in their business pitches. The principles are embodied in a simple list of five promises about our business: Client Focus, Respect for the Individual, Teamwork, Responsible Citizenship, and Integrity.

The unwritten principle that I stressed to all employees was to not be afraid to fail. In teaching the Merrill Lynch training class, I would always make certain that someone asked me the secret of success. My answer is "a willingness to expose yourself to failure."

I give the example that when Babe Ruth led the major leagues in home runs, he also led the league in strikeouts. People remember that. Ty Cobb stole 96 bases one year, but that was in 130 attempts, meaning his success rate was only about

> It's only when we develop others that we permanently succeed.

75 percent. The man who was second that year stole 78 bases in 80 attempts. Nobody remembers his name. His percentage was a lot higher, but he didn't take enough chances to really make himself successful.

The message is clear: If you want to be a leader, not just another face in the crowd, you have to take those extra chances.

ALFRED P. WEST JR.

While I was a student at the Wharton School of Business at the University of Pennsylvania, one of my professors used simulators to train the students in his class. He set up mock companies on computers, and teams of students competed against other teams as if they were operating in the "real world."

The simulators were similar to those that had been used for training airline pilots for years. As I went through that class, I kept having a recurring thought—if training pilots on simulators is successful, and we are using simulators in this class to learn how to run a business, what other ways could simulators be used?

Part of my interest stemmed from the fact that I was an aeronautical engineer by training, having earned my undergraduate degree in that subject at Georgia Tech. I had planned to fly fighters for the air force, but declined my commission because of problems with my eyesight.

Instead, I enrolled at Wharton, and the experience in that class formed the basis for what would become my life's work. My father had worked for a large insurance company before going to work for himself, and he had taught me how working for yourself was always the best way to go if you had a choice.

The idea of using simulators in business prompted me to form a company, SEI, with the express purpose of developing sim-

© Amos Chan, NYC

AL WEST founded SEI in 1968 while he was a student at the
Wharton School of Business. The company's first product was
a training simulator sold to banks, and his firm was instrumen-
tal in the automation of bank services. A graduate of Georgia
Tech with a degree in aerospace engineering, West earned his
MBA at Wharton.

ulator training for businesses. I became so immersed in the company that I didn't even finish my doctorate dissertation at Wharton after earning my MBA in 1967, forming SEI in 1968.

Of course it takes more than a good idea to make a new business successful. During World War II, my father had been a roommate of Tom Gates, the Secretary of Defense under President Eisenhower and then the chairman of Morgan Guaranty, the top bank in the country. He was able to include our company in a small business investment corporation, and that allowed us to get some early venture capital funding.

Having that connection opened the door for us and provided us instant credibility. Here I was, at 23 or 24 years old, and nobody knew anything about me, but they knew about Tom Gates and Morgan Guaranty and that prompted those banks to take a chance on us.

Our first client was a bank. The officer there had written a government proposal for high schools and was trying to get a new business off the ground. We were able to

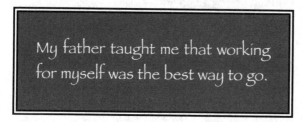

My father taught me that working for myself was the best way to go.

hook up with him and began training his loan officers. We simulated case studies in commercial credit, and taught cash flow.

The success of that program led us into agreements with other banks, and we were able to build a real-time loan system. After that program was started, we expanded again when we found a need from the trust departments of banks to write a computer system to do portfolios and client accounting.

All of our eventually led us into a business where we essentially went around automating the back rooms of banks. We happened to be starting this business right in the middle of a recession, and the only companies that had money were banks. Between 1971 and 1981, we were able to automate 35 percent of the banks in the United States.

Our business has continued to evolve from that point. We took SEI public in 1981 to get the venture capital firm out, and entered the mutual funds business by automating trust cash management. Two years later, we entered the pension plan investment consulting area.

Now, we have kind of reinvented the company the last three years to cover almost all aspects of asset management and financial planning, or financial wellness.

One of the lessons I have learned since forming the business is that the success of any business is very much determined by the relationships established between the company and its clients. A company could have a great business model, but if the employees are not able to interact as people, then the company is not going to be successful. The companies that focus so much on their products because they are always chasing the money, and less time developing those solid relationships, are the ones which more often than not struggle.

Because my father was in the insurance business, he taught

> Don't spend time on anything your customers aren't interested in.

me all about the importance of developing solid business relationships. That is often times all you have to differentiate yourself from other companies.

ARTHUR L. WILLIAMS

From an early age, I wanted to grow up and be a high school football coach, just like my daddy and Tommy Taylor, who became the recreation director in my hometown of Cairo, Georgia when I was 11 years old. Coach Taylor had more influence on my early years than everyone else I came into contact with combined.

Coach Taylor gave me my first job—I earned 25 cents a night to sit in center field at the local baseball park and hang wooden scorecards on nails during the games, and then to clean up the ballpark after everyone had gone home. There was nothing electronic at the baseball park in 1953.

Coach Taylor was hired as the head track coach and basketball coach at the local high school and over the next 18 years won 12 state championships in track and two back-to-back state championships in basketball. To him, there was no excuse for being disorganized. He was so fanatical that he was known to stay up all night planning strategy for track meets.

He held everyone who played for him to the same high standards and drew out unprecedented performances from his players. He is the reason I went to Mississippi State University in Starkville, Mississippi, on a full football scholarship. My dreams were set; I was going to get my degree in physical education and come back home to coach.

ART WILLIAMS thought he would spend his life as a high school football coach, then as a principal. A conversation with a relative, however, started Williams on a different journey, one that resulted in the creation of the A.L. Williams Co., which became the largest life insurance company in the United States in only 12 years. A graduate of Mississippi State University with a master's degree from Auburn, Williams is now retired. He is the author of three books, including *Pushing Up People*. Williams and his wife, Angela, have two children and seven grandchildren.

When I was a junior, however, my father died of a heart attack at the age of 48. He had a good job as the head chemist of the Roddenberry pickle factory, but he never made more than $10,000 a year. He left my mother and three children with no will, no meaningful savings and very little life insurance. My mother, who had never worked outside the home, all of a sudden had to find a way to support her family.

I was already married with a one-year-old child and was self-sufficient. My wife, Angela, and I helped my mother as much as we could, but the next few years were long and rough for her. That was a lesson that was going to prove very meaningful to me later in my life.

After graduation, my dream came true and I became the offensive and defensive backfield coach at Thomasville High School, 12 miles from Cairo. Two years later, I was hired as the head coach at Appling County High School in Baxley, Georgia, and it turned out to be a major challenge.

The school had not had a winning season in 20 years,

> Have passion in all you do! Win with your heart, not your head.

and at the end of spring tryouts I had only 19 boys on the team and we were playing in one of the toughest football regions in Georgia. We beat the number one-ranked team in the state and won seven out of our 10 games. I was voted Coach of the Year. We accomplished this by outworking our competition and always doing "a little bit more"—if our competition worked one hour in the weight room, we worked an hour and 30 minutes. After a second winning season, I was itching for a bigger challenge and moved on to Kendrick High School in Columbus, a new school.

Over Thanksgiving, I went to a family reunion. My accountant cousin, Ted Harrison, told me he had started selling term insurance and investments part-time with a company called ITT. When we looked at my situation, I was stunned. Angela and I were paying $20 a month for a $15,000 whole life insurance policy. Ted explained that if I died, Angela would get $15,000, less than two years' income. That was exactly what had happened to my mother.

Ted showed me that for the same $20 a month, I could buy $150,000 of term life protection. I had never heard of term protection. He explained it was nothing more than pure death protection. Most companies didn't sell it because it was an inexpensive product and offered only a small profit to the company and low commissions to the agent.

I was furious, because I knew my dad had probably never known he had a better choice. The more I thought about it, I didn't think that could be right. I started investigating myself—I found out Ted was absolutely correct.

I began telling everyone I met about what I had learned, and I found out everyone was in the same situation. Nobody had heard of term insurance. I was still mad three weeks later, when I attended a PTA meeting. It was only the second time in my career, I think, that I had gone to a PTA meeting.

A man named Forest Smith was there and he introduced himself to me. He told me he was the division manager for ITT Financial Services. I almost dropped my Coke. I told him about Ted and my father—and before I knew it I had begun working for ITT part-time.

I hated sales, and the last thing I wanted to be was a salesman, but the concept of "Buy Term and Invest the Difference" was so intriguing I couldn't stop thinking or talking about it. My crusade was simple: to tell people about term insurance and show them what a ripoff cash value life insurance was.

I made my first sale four months after the family reunion and made $325. For the next two and a half years, I worked on a part-time basis and saved $42,000 from my insurance sales.

Our football team was having great success as well, but what caught the attention of Frank Pierson, president of ITT, was my sales success. Working part-time, I was making more money in six months than most of his full-time sales people were making in a year. I tried to convince him the key was that I was not a salesman, and he needed to hire more part-time people like me to work for him.

Frank finally bought on to what I was saying, offering me $25,000 a year to see if I could build on the part-time concept—but he told me I had to quit coaching football to do it. He was offering me the same kind of opportunity I had received coaching football, a chance to build a new kind of team with my own concepts. As much as I was intrigued, I didn't want to give up my dream of coaching. I spent the next four months agonizing over the decision.

The more I thought about it, the more excited I got and I knew it was the right decision. I knew my idea would work. Still, I needed one more opinion. I got in my car and drove to Cairo to talk to Coach Taylor.

After I explained the situation to him, his reasoning was simple: "Art, if you feel like this could be big in business, then you really ought to do it," he said. "You've been a success in coaching. Nobody can take that away from you. All kinds of schools would give their right arm to have you come coach for them. If this doesn't work out, you haven't lost anything. Go for it."

I took Coach Taylor's advice, and it turned out I was right. My "experiment" of hiring part-timers was a blazing success. When ITT began having financial difficulties, I took most of my sales force with me to Waddell & Reed. After three years, they were also struggling, so I made the decision to plunge out on my own.

On February 10, 1977, with 85 people, we opened the doors to what would become A.L. Williams and took on the life insurance industry. We were on a mission, and by 1984 we had become the number-one producer of individual life insurance in the industry, beating Prudential, New York Life and 2,000 other companies. Two years later, nine years after we opened our doors, A.L. Williams out-produced the second- and third-place companies combined. We sold $92.3 billion worth of insurance, New York Life sold $46.4 billion and Prudential sold $36.3 billion.

In 12 years, A.L. Williams had grown to a workforce of 225,000 people and had become the only $300 billion life insurance company in history.

The secret to our success was simple: We put the consumer first—our concept of "Buy Term and Invest the Difference" is the best way to protect your family. The second reason for our success is that we had a passion about what we were doing. I believe you win with your heart, not with your head. I've always believed that other company's agents sold life insurance to "make a living," while A.L. Williams people sold life insurance to "correct an injustice." What a powerful advantage.

Not only did we become the largest life insurance company in history, but our people 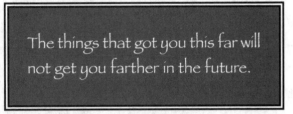 had unbelievable financial success. A $10,000 investment in the original A.L. Williams stock in 1981 was worth more than $6,210,000 in 2001—a return of 62,707 percent!

The things that got you this far will not get you farther in the future.

I've always said the scoreboard tells the story. In 1989, when we sold the company, the average death benefit paid by A.L. Williams was $100,000. Prudential's average was $4,500 and the average for the entire industry was $6,000.

My philosophy for building a company was "Pushing Up People," which I used as the title of a book I wrote. Coaching was all I knew. I never considered myself a boss. I was the coach. A boss has a way of making you feel bad. Coaches make you feel special. A coach looks for strengths and good qualities. A boss tries to motivate by threats and intimidation. There is a big difference.